AF228460

SERIES ENDORSEMENTS

"There are so many fine commentaries available today, but it's great to have a reliable author you can turn to for solid Reformed reflections on Scripture. In this case, the authors are friends and fellow shepherds who have given me great insight into God's Word over the years. I'm looking forward eagerly to each one of these sermonic commentaries!"

Michael S. Horton
J. Gresham Machen Professor of Apologetics and Systematic Theology at Westminster Seminary California
Host of the *White Horse Inn* Talk Show
Editor-in-Chief of *Modern Reformation* magazine

"Those of us who have promoted and practiced *lectio continua* expository preaching through the years eagerly await the volumes announced in The *Lectio Continua* Expository Commentary on the New Testament. We are equally eager to read such a series written by pastors who have practiced the method in their churches. The international and interdenominational character of the series will only add to the richness of its insights."

T. David Gordon
Professor of Religion and Greek at Grove City College
Author of *Why Johnny Can't Preach*

"As the history of preaching is unfolded, it becomes clear how important the orderly, systematic preaching through the Scriptures has been, and why it has been a favorite homiletic approach over the centuries. One is surprised to discover how many of history's great preachers made a regular practice of preaching through one book of the Bible after another. Origen, the first Christian preacher from whom we have any sizable collection of sermons, preached most of his sermons on the *lectio continua.* We find the same with John Chrysostom who is usually referred to as the greatest Christian preacher. We find the same true of Augustine as well. At the time of the Protestant Reformation, Zwingli, Calvin, Bucer, and Knox followed this system regularly, and they passed it on to the Puritans. Today, we see a real revival of *lectio continua* preaching. The *Lectio Continua* Expository Commentary on the New Testament represents a wonderful opportunity for the Church to recover a truly expository pulpit."

Hughes Oliphant Old
Formerly John H. Leith Professor of Reformed Theology and Worship at Erskine Theological Seminary
Author of *The Reading and Preaching of the Scriptures in the Worship of the Christian Church* (7 vols., Eerdmans, 2007)

"The concept behind this series is a fascinating one and, given the list of authors, I am confident that the final product will not disappoint. This promises to be a great resource for churches seeking to know the Word of God more fully."

Carl R. Trueman
Professor of Biblical and Religious Studies at Grove City College

Titus and Philemon

THE *LECTIO CONTINUA*
EXPOSITORY COMMENTARY ON THE NEW TESTAMENT

Series Editors

Joel R. Beeke | Jon D. Payne

Available books in this series:

Romans — J. V. Fesko
First Corinthians — Kim Riddlebarger
Galatians — J. V. Fesko
Ephesians — Ian Hamilton
Philippians — David T. A. Strain
Second Timothy — Michael G. Brown
Titus and Philemon — Malcolm Maclean
Hebrews — David B. McWilliams
Revelation — Joel R. Beeke

Titus and Philemon

Malcolm Maclean

REFORMATION HERITAGE BOOKS
Grand Rapids, Michigan

Titus and Philemon

Reformation Heritage Books
3070 29th St. SE
Grand Rapids, MI 49512
616-977-0889
orders@heritagebooks.org
www.heritagebooks.org

Printed in the United States of America
24 25 26 27 28 29/10 9 8 7 6 5 4 3 2 1

Library of Congress Cataloging-in-Publication Data

Names: Maclean, Malcolm, Rev., author.
Title: Titus and Philemon / Malcolm Maclean.
Description: Grand Rapids, Michigan : Reformation Heritage Books, [2024] | Series: The Lectio Continua expository commentary on the New Testament | Includes bibliographical references.
Identifiers: LCCN 2024021567 (print) | LCCN 2024021568 (ebook) | ISBN 9798886861303 (hardcover) | ISBN 9798886861310 (epub)
Subjects: LCSH: Bible. Titus—Commentaries. | Bible. Philemon—Commentaries.
Classification: LCC BS2755.53 .M33 2024 (print) | LCC BS2755.53 (ebook) | DDC 227/.85—dc23/eng/20240607
LC record available at https://lccn.loc.gov/2024021567
LC ebook record available at https://lccn.loc.gov/2024021568

Contents

St. Peter's Church in Heidelberg, Germany, where Caspar Olevianus pastored and proclaimed God's Word in 1562

Series Introduction

The greatest need of the church today is the recovery of sound biblical preaching. We need preaching that faithfully explains and applies the text, courageously confronts sin, and boldly trumpets forth the sovereign majesty, law, and gospel promises of God. This type of powerful proclamation has vanished in many quarters of the evangelical church only to be replaced by that which is anemic and man-centered. Instead of doctrinally rich exposition which strengthens faith and fosters Christian maturity, the standard fare has become informal, chatty, anecdote-laden messages, devoid of instruction in the truths of the Christian faith. This approach leaves unbelievers confused and keeps believers in a state of chronic spiritual adolescence.[1]

There is indeed a dire need for the recovery of solid biblical preaching. Not only does reformation of this sort lead Christ's sheep back to the verdant pastures of His soul-nourishing word, it also provides a good example for present and future generations

---

1. A stinging, yet constructive critique of modern-day preaching is found in T. David Gordon's *Why Johnny Can't Preach: The Media Have Shaped the Messengers* (Phillipsburg, N.J.: P&R, 2009). "I have come to recognize that many, many individuals today have never been under a steady diet of competent preaching.... As starving children in Manila sift through the landfill for food, Christians in many churches today have never experienced genuine soul-nourishing preaching, and so they just pick away at what is available to them, trying to find a morsel of spiritual sustenance or helpful counsel here or there" (17). Elements of this introduction are adapted from Jon D. Payne, "The Roaring of Christ through *Lectio Continua* Preaching," *Modern Reformation* 19, no. 6 (Nov.–Dec. 2010): 23–24, and are used by permission of the publisher.

of ministers. For this reason, we are pleased to introduce The *Lectio Continua* Expository Commentary on the New Testament, a new series of expository commentaries authored by an array of seasoned pastor-scholars from various Reformed denominations on both sides of the Atlantic.

What is the *lectio continua* method of preaching?[2] It is simply the uninterrupted, systematic, expository proclamation of God's word—verse by verse, chapter by chapter, book by book—that endeavors to deliver the whole counsel of God (Acts 20:26–27). Christian discipleship is impoverished when large portions of Scripture are ignored. Carried out faithfully, the *lectio continua* method ensures that every passage is mined for its riches (even those verses which are obscure, controversial, or hard to swallow). Paul states that "all scripture is given by inspiration of God, and is profitable for doctrine, for reproof, for correction, for instruction in righteousness: that the man of God may be perfect, thoroughly furnished unto all good works" (2 Tim. 3:16–17 KJV).

Lectio continua preaching has a splendid heritage. It finds its roots in the early church and patristic eras. Its use, however, was revived and greatly expanded during the sixteenth-century Protestant Reformation. When Huldrych Zwingli (d. 1531) arrived at the Zurich Grossmunster in 1519, it was his desire to dispense with the standard lectionary[3] and introduce *lectio continua* preaching to his congregation by moving systematically through the Gospel of Matthew. At first, some members of his church council were suspicious. They were uncomfortable replacing the lectionary with this

2. In Christianity, *lectio continua* (Latin for "continuous reading") originally referred to the practice of reading Scripture sequentially in public worship, as was the practice of the ancient church. This practice is recommended by the Westminster divines in the Directory for Public Worship, which in turn served as an impetus for *lectio continua* preaching. Sadly, Scripture reading in this manner has been neglected in Reformed and Presbyterian churches for many generations, perhaps as far back as the eighteenth century, when public worship was reduced to sermon-hearing sessions.

3. A *lectionary* is a plan or table of Scripture passages to be read in the services of church for each day or week of the year.

seemingly new approach. But Zwingli explained that the *lectio continua* method of preaching was not new at all. On the contrary, important figures such as Augustine (d. 430), Chrysostom (d. 407), and Bernard of Clairvaux (d. 1153) employed this homiletical approach. Zwingli is quoted by his successor, Heinrich Bullinger (d. 1575), as saying that "no friend of evangelical truth could have any reason to complain" about such a method.[4]

Zwingli rightly believed that the quickest way to restore biblical Christianity to the church was to preach the whole counsel of God verse by verse, chapter by chapter, book by book, Lord's Day after Lord's Day, year after year. Other Reformers agreed and followed his pattern. In the city of Strasbourg, just ninety miles north of Zurich, preachers such as Martin Bucer (d. 1551), Wolfgang Capito (d. 1570), and Kaspar Hedio (d. 1552) practiced *lectio continua* preaching. Johannes Oecolampadius (d. 1531) boldly preached the *lectio continua* in Basel. And let us not forget John Calvin (d. 1564); between 1549 and 1564, the Genevan Reformer preached sequentially through no fewer than twenty-five books of the Bible (over two thousand sermons), which he was able to do because he also preached regularly for weekday services.[5]

The example of these Reformers has been emulated by preachers throughout the centuries, from the post-Reformation age down to the present. In the last half of the twentieth century, Donald Grey Barnhouse (1895–1960), Martyn Lloyd-Jones (d. 1981), William Still (d. 1997), James Montgomery Boice (d. 2000), and John MacArthur boldly preached straight through books of the Bible from their pulpits. But why? Surely we have acquired better, more

4. It is interesting to note that the year before Zwingli began preaching sequentially through books of the Bible, he had received a new edition of Chrysostom's *lectio continua* sermons on Matthew's Gospel. See Hughes Oliphant Old, *The Patristic Roots of Reformed Worship* (Black Mountain, N.C.: Worship Press, 2004), 195. Cf. Hughes Oliphant Old, *The Reading and Preaching of the Scriptures in the Worship of the Christian Church,* vol. 4: *The Age of the Reformation* (Grand Rapids: Eerdmans, 2002); and Timothy George, *Reading Scripture with the Reformers* (Downers Grove, Ill.: IVP Academic, 2011), 228–53.

5. T. H. L. Parker, *Calvin's Preaching* (Edinburgh: T&T Clark, 1992), 159.

contemporary methods of preaching. Is the *lectio continua* relevant in our twenty-first century context? In a day when biblical preaching is being increasingly undermined and marginalized by media/story/therapy/personality-driven sermons, even among the avowedly Reformed, these are important questions to consider.

Shortly before the apostle Paul was martyred in Rome by Emperor Nero, he penned 2 Timothy. In what proved to be some of his final words to his young disciple, he wrote, "I charge thee therefore before God, and the Lord Jesus Christ…*preach the word*; be instant in season, out of season; reprove, rebuke, exhort with all longsuffering and doctrine" (2 Tim. 4:1–2 KJV; emphasis added). This directive was not meant only for Timothy. It is the duty of every Christian minister (and church) to heed these timeless words; according to God's divine blueprint for ministry, it is chiefly through the faithful proclamation of the word that Christ saves, sanctifies, and comforts the beloved church for which He died.[6] In other words, the preaching of the gospel and the right administration of the sacraments are the divinely sanctioned and efficacious means by which Christ and all His benefits of redemption are communicated to the elect. For this reason alone, the *lectio continua* method of preaching is a helpful practice in our churches, providing a steady diet of law and gospel from the entirety of God's word.

Some may ask, "Why another expository commentary series?" First, because in every generation it is highly valuable to provide fresh and reliable expositions of God's word. Every age possesses its own set of theological, ecclesiastical, and cultural challenges. Thus, it is beneficial for both current and rising ministers in every generation to have trustworthy contemporary models of biblical preaching. Second, these volumes uniquely feature the expositions of an array of pastors from a variety of Reformed and confessional traditions. Consequently, this series brings a wealth of exegetical, confessional,

6. See Matthew 28:18–20; Romans 10:14–17; 1 Corinthians 1:18–21; 1 Peter 1:22–25; Westminster Shorter Catechism, Q. 89.

experiential, and practical insight and furnishes the reader with an instructive and stimulating selection of *lectio continua* sermons.

This series is not meant to be an academic or highly technical commentary. There are many helpful exegetical commentaries written for that purpose. Rather, the aim is to provide *lectio continua* sermons, originally delivered to Reformed congregations, which clearly and faithfully communicate the context, meaning, gravity, and application of God's inerrant word. Each volume of expositions aspires to be redemptive-historical, covenantal, Reformed and confessional, Trinitarian, Christ-centered, and teeming with spiritual and practical application. Therefore, we pray that the series will be a profound blessing to every Christian believer who longs to "grow in grace, and in the knowledge of our Lord and Saviour Jesus Christ" (2 Peter 3:18 KJV).

We are pleased to announce that this series of commentaries is now being published by Reformation Heritage Books, who have graciously agreed to take over this large task from *Tolle Lege* Press. We thank *Tolle Lege* for printing the first three volumes (*First Corinthians* by Kim Riddlebarger, *Galatians* by John Fesko, and *Hebrews* by David McWilliams). We, Jon Payne and Joel Beeke, look forward to coediting the remainder of the series for Reformation Heritage Books. The goal is to publish two volumes per year using the King James or New King James Version, according to the choice of each author.

In addition to thanking Reformation Heritage Books and its faithful team for producing this series, we wish to thank our churches, Christ Church Presbyterian, Charleston, South Carolina, and the Heritage Reformed Congregation, Grand Rapids, Michigan, for warmly encouraging us as ministers to work on projects such as this one that impact the wider church. Furthermore, we thank our dear wives, Marla Payne and Mary Beeke, and our precious children, for their heartwarming support, which makes editing a series like this one possible. We both feel that God has greatly blessed us with God-fearing wives and children who mean more to us than words can express.

Finally, and most importantly, thanks and praise must be given to our blessed triune God, the eternal Fountain of all grace and truth. By His sovereign love and mercy and through faith in the crucified, resurrected, and ascended Christ, we have been "born again, not of corruptible seed, but of incorruptible, by the word of God, which liveth and abideth for ever. For all flesh is as grass, and all the glory of man as the flower of grass. The grass withereth, and the flower thereof falleth away: but the word of the Lord endureth for ever. And this is the word which by the gospel is preached unto you" (1 Peter 1:23–25 KJV).

—Jon D. Payne and Joel R. Beeke, series editors

Titus

Introduction to Titus

There are other commentaries that deal with background aspects of Paul's letter to Titus in great depth, and they provide insights into the possible circumstances behind it. Most experts accept that the letter was written between Paul's two imprisonments in Rome when he was released for a time during the AD 60s. During this period, he also wrote 1 and 2 Timothy, probably writing his letter to Titus between them. If this scenario is correct, the letters were written during Paul's fourth missionary journey.

It is not possible to say where Paul was when he sent the letter to Titus. The only information he gives about his circumstances is that he intends to go to Nicopolis for the winter and asks Titus to meet him there once a replacement has been found for him in Crete (Titus 3:12). There was more than one city with that name, and Paul does not indicate which one he is referring to.

In this brief introduction, I will give details about two questions. One is why Paul left Titus in Crete, and the other concerns who Titus was.

Why Did Paul Leave Titus in Crete?

Paul left Titus in Crete to focus on the growth of the new churches he and Titus had founded. Paul indicates that churches had been planted in every town (1:5). Crete had about a hundred locations that could be described as towns, so Paul may be saying that a church now existed in each location. If that was the case, then Titus had a lot of work to do. But the verse may mean only that Titus had been asked to develop churches in several locations.

The task for Titus included appointing elders, dealing with the adverse influence of false teachers, guiding households about internal relationships, ensuring a right attitude to the civil authorities, and understanding the importance of good works in daily life. Paul did not expect Titus to be in Crete for a prolonged period (3:12).

People from Crete were present on the day of Pentecost (Acts 2:11), but about thirty years had passed since then. No indication is given in the letter to Titus whether any of them were still in Crete or even if they had made any impression for the gospel there before the visit of Paul and Titus.

Clearly, the onset of new Christian churches will have different arrangements from established churches until the new congregations become stable. In a situation such as existed in Crete, Paul and Titus would have to plan for how the congregations they planted would become viable and reliable witnesses in their communities. Paul could have sent in a team if he thought it was necessary, but he obviously thought that leaving Titus there would be enough. So Titus was given the task.

Who Was Titus?

Although Titus was with Paul during periods described in the book of Acts, he is not referred to by its author, Luke. Instead, Titus is mentioned by Paul in four of his letters; in addition to this personal letter, Titus is also mentioned in Galatians, 2 Corinthians, and 2 Timothy, and each of these references reveal that he was crucial at times in helping Paul's ministry.

Titus and the Circumcision Debate

The reference to Titus in Galatians indicates that he was involved with Paul from the early days of his missionary travels since the letter was written between the first and second of Paul's three missionary journeys mentioned in Acts. In Acts 15 Luke mentions how several men from the church in Antioch were sent to Jerusalem to discuss the question of Gentile circumcision. Luke says only that Paul and Barnabas and some others were sent. Paul, however, says in Galatians 2:3 that Titus was with them on that occasion. He also says that Titus became a cause of controversy because he had not been circumcised. Paul refused to allow Titus to be circumcised because he was a Gentile and not a Jew.

Titus and the Corinthian Church

Titus then is absent from the biblical account for several years. He is mentioned next in 2 Corinthians, and in it he is referred to several times. Paul had sent him to Corinth to deal with important issues sadly taking place in the church there, such as allowing immoral practices and other wrong behaviors that Paul deals with in 1 Corinthians. Titus had returned to Paul with a good report of the repentance of the Corinthians and informed the apostle that their penitent actions had refreshed his spirit (2 Cor. 7:13–15).

In addition, Titus had been involved in a great collection that Paul was arranging for the needy Christians in Jerusalem (2 Cor. 8:6). Paul, therefore, urged him to return to Corinth and complete the task, which he was willing to do, thus revealing his love for the Corinthians (vv. 16–18). Probably, he also carried 2 Corinthians when he went back to Corinth.

While it is difficult to work out all the historical details Paul mentions, it is clear that Titus made two trips to Corinth in order to help the church there. One visit was to deal with the problems in the church, and the other was to help with the collection that Paul was arranging. Those visits must have been demanding physically, but Titus was willing to make them.

Titus and Crete

Paul does not mention Titus again for another few years, until he writes to him this letter about the visit they had made to Crete. He then left Titus in Crete to help the churches that had been started there (Titus 1:5). It was Paul's intention to send either Artemis or Tychicus to relieve Titus so that he could rejoin Paul (3:12). Paul's descriptions of the Cretans are not flattering, so we can imagine that Titus would have faced some difficulties as he worked to establish those fledgling churches.

Titus and Dalmatia

The final mention of Titus is in 2 Timothy 4:10. In that verse, Paul says that he has sent Titus to Dalmatia (located in modern Croatia), although he does not say why, but it was probably related to church matters there. How long he stayed there cannot now be known. Eusebius, the church historian of the fourth century, says that Titus eventually made his way back to Crete, but that claim cannot be proved.

As we reflect on these brief mentions of Titus in Paul's letters, we can see that he was no ordinary man. That Paul sent him to deal with difficult problems in the churches in Corinth and Crete tells us that he was capable of dealing effectively with people who had strong opinions and who would have resisted attempts to change them. In those situations, Paul did not merely want to win an argument. He wanted those who had fallen to be restored and those who had been misled returned to the right way. The man to do this was Titus, and this tells us that he had a very strong pastoral heart. With regard to the church in Corinth, he had rejoiced to see their spiritual restoration. And that eventually he was able to leave Crete points to his having achieved Paul's purpose for the churches there as well. It is not surprising that Paul earlier called him "my partner and fellow worker concerning you" (2 Cor. 8:23).

1

Paul, a Man on a Mission

TITUS 1:1a

[1a]Paul, a bondservant of God and an apostle of Jesus Christ, according to…God's elect.

Paul is one of the most famous individuals in history. If we were to poll people and ask them to name two or three Bible characters, they probably would mention Paul. They might not know much else about him, but at least they would know his name. Yet if we were also to ask why they know about Paul, some people might say that he was someone who served Jesus Christ and also wrote some of the books of the Bible. In a way, that answer sums up his life after his conversion.

Earlier in his life, Paul would have caused a lot of fear for some people. Back then, he may not have been known as Paul but only as Saul of Tarsus. It was customary for Jewish individuals in that period to have more than one name, so even then he could have been addressed as either Saul or Paul. Or maybe he assumed the name Paul later.[1] Whatever the source of his name, he was a very strong opponent of Jesus Christ and showed his opposition by determining to harass and punish any of his countrymen who accepted that Jesus was the Messiah.

1. It has been observed that in the book of Acts, Luke does not refer to him as Paul until the incident when Sergius Paulus was converted (13:7–12), leading some to wonder if that conversion in some way led him to adopt the name Paul.

It was while Paul was attempting to deal with those Christians that he came into direct contact with Jesus. The meeting happened on a journey to Damascus, where some Jewish believers in Jesus lived. Before that meeting, Paul probably had met many important people, such as leaders in the Jewish community in Jerusalem or prominent Roman politicians or military persons. But those encounters paled into complete insignificance once he had met Jesus. Paul's first response to Jesus indicated that was the case because he asked, "Who are You, Lord?" (Acts 9:5). He had realized that the one speaking to him was none other than God. He was likely astonished when the speaker from heaven then revealed that He was Jesus, and Paul was fighting against Him.

Have you ever met an important person? I don't mean that you merely saw such an individual. Rather, have you had the opportunity to spend time with a well-known individual that altered your opinion of him or her and of yourself? Maybe that person was a politician, and after meeting and listening to her, you decided to vote for her. Perhaps you joined the political party that she represented. Or maybe you met a soccer player, and after being in his company for a short time, you decided that soccer was the sport for you.

We all have life-changing encounters. If you are a man, you probably have met many women in your social circle or in your work, but you were not drawn romantically to them. Then one day you met a woman to whom you were attracted, and the more you came to know of her, the more she affected your life. Meeting her changed your life, and you would not be where you are now if you had not met her. Love for her directed your future.

In a spiritual way, Paul, on the road to Damascus, discovered that life had a different road for him. When he took his first steps on it, he did not know exactly where it would take him. Jesus did say to him,

> I am Jesus, whom you are persecuting. But rise and stand on your feet; for I have appeared to you for this purpose, to make you a minister and a witness both of the things which you have seen and of the things which I will yet reveal to you. I

> will deliver you from the Jewish people, as well as from the Gentiles, to whom I now send you, to open their eyes, in order to turn them from darkness to light, and from the power of Satan to God, that they may receive forgiveness of sins and an inheritance among those who are sanctified by faith in Me. (Acts 26:15–18)

Paul had been fulfilling this purpose ever since that notable meeting. It was the reason why he had been in Crete with Titus. About thirty years had passed since he had first met Jesus, and during that time he had taken the gospel to numerous places and seen many people become Christians. This was the case in Crete as well. It seemed that wherever he went, no matter the people group—and some of them initially seemed very unlikely converts—he knew gospel success. This had been the case even in situations where he had known much physical suffering for his faith.

Such an experience as Paul had calls us to further thought. Why did Paul want to serve Jesus for such a long time? Why did he know such success in his endeavors? What was the message he taught that resulted in such effects? Who did he think he was as he engaged in such activities? His words in the opening section of his letter to Titus answer some of these questions, so we will consider how he described himself.

Paul's Description of Himself

Sometimes when people go for employment interviews, they are asked to describe themselves in a few words. The reason for such a question is to find out what makes them do the things they do. If a job applicant says he plays golf frequently, the interviewer could assume he enjoys playing that game. The interviewer could also assume that he loves taking part in that sport and could even conclude that he would introduce others to the game and encourage them to join in. A simple question leads to answers that reveal a great deal.

Imagine Paul at such an interview. The interviewer says, "Paul, tell us about yourself in a few words." He replies, "I am a bondservant of God and an apostle of Jesus Christ." We can see the interviewer lifting up his head from his notes with a look that says he realizes that the one he is interviewing is not an ordinary person. In fact, he may suspect that before him is someone exceptionally unusual.

So how do we react when we read that Paul is a bondservant of God and an apostle of Jesus Christ? Certainly, he is making astonishing claims for himself. Someone who would make these assertions is either very sure of who he is or is totally deluded. But when we consider other letters that Paul has written, we find that he is consistent in his self-understanding. His self-knowledge does not make him proud, nor does he deny that he is still a great sinner. Nowhere does he show signs that he is confused as to his identity. Instead, he clearly says what he does and for whom he does it.

Perhaps we don't know exactly what Paul means when he calls himself a bondservant and an apostle. The term "servant" is used in many ways in everyday life. We may have heard or read the term "apostle" used with a religious connection but never realized what it means. So let us think briefly about the words "bondservant" and "apostle."

The word translated "bondservant" is *doulos*, which means "a slave." Paul's Master is God, which is a way of saying that he serves devotedly the Father in heaven and also recognizes that the Father has complete authority over him. Such a way of speaking reveals that Paul is both diligent in his role and pleased with it. If he had resented the Father's authority, he would not have wanted to be identified as His servant.

In addition, Paul was aware that the title "servant of God" had a long history in the nation of Israel, describing those whom God had called to a special task. Those who spoke on God's behalf in the Old Testament—that is, the prophets—were called by this title. Paul was consciously identifying himself with those who had a special divine calling to communicate God's will. Many of Paul's listeners were Jews, and they would have recognized what Paul was claiming whenever he said that he was a bondservant of God. And we can see later in the letter that Jews living in Crete had heard Paul when he was there.

In saying that he was an apostle of Jesus Christ, Paul saw himself as a special messenger of the One he had met on the road to Damascus. The message that he declared was that Jesus was the promised Messiah, the Christ, described many times in Old Testament prophecies. In order to be this special messenger, Paul had to have seen Jesus risen from the dead (Acts 1:22), which had happened when Jesus interrupted Paul's plans to visit Damascus. Paul had been called by the risen Jesus, even as His original disciples had been, to take the gospel to the world (Matt. 28:18–20).

Yet we should not read Paul's self-description and assume that there is no application for us. Just because we are not such bondservants or apostles does not mean that we should not be challenged by his dedication. In another letter he expresses his understanding of life when he writes, "For to me, to live is Christ" (Phil. 1:21). What mattered to Paul was giving God the Father the honor that He is due and giving to Jesus the place that He deserves in the life of His messengers. Paul was not perfect, but he was devoted, and we can all be that, whether we are pastors, elders, deacons, or laypeople. In fact, we should be that devoted. And Paul goes on to say why.

Paul's Concern

Why did Paul serve in such a manner? What was required of him as a bondservant and an apostle? The role for which he was selected and sent was all about those he describes as God's elect. Who did Paul have in mind? He was thinking of all those who had responded to the gospel by repenting of their sins and believing in Jesus. He would also include all who had trusted in God with saving faith since the beginning of time and those who would yet believe in such a manner in the centuries ahead. But why does he regard believers as God's elect? Because he knew that without God's prior election of them, they would not have believed in Jesus.

Election can be a troubling topic for people because they think it makes God unfair or unjust. Yet that is to make assumptions about God's reasons for choosing His people. The best way to find out why someone does something is to consider what their motives are in doing it. Why did God choose His people? He says that He did so because He loved them (Eph. 1:4–5). Whatever else we wish to make of divine election, we cannot deny that it is an expression of divine love. Moreover, we cannot identify the objects of God's love until they reveal that they have believed the gospel. The gospel is a message of love, of divine love for sinners, that involved the Father sending His Son to die on the cross for them.

When we think about divine election, it is important to do so according to what God has revealed about it. Election is not a barrier to conversions; rather, it is a guarantee of conversions. Neither is it a hindrance to assurance of salvation; rather, it is a confirmation that salvation is guaranteed. There are some Christians who deny sovereign election, but they have not been more successful about converting everyone than have those who affirm election. And it is very comforting to discover that the God who provides spiritual blessings in this life to those who believe the gospel had an eternal plan to do so.

Earlier in his ministry, when Paul had arrived in Corinth for the first time as an apostle, he became discouraged. Luke does not mention the exact causes of the discouragement in his account of what Paul experienced at that time. He does, however, say that God encouraged His fearful servant by reminding him that because of the reality of election, he would know success, even in Corinth. Through a vision God told Paul, "Do not be afraid, but speak, and do not keep silent; for I am with you, and no one will attack you to hurt you; for I have many people in this city" (Acts 18:9–10). Those people were not yet converted, but nothing could prevent them from becoming Christians, not even strong opposition. And that was a great comfort for Paul, and he continued to work there for another eighteen months.

It is the case that Corinth was known throughout the ancient world for its sinfulness. So, too, was Crete. As Paul begins his letter to Titus, who is laboring for Jesus on the island, he mentions the reality that God has an elect people. Some Cretans had already come to faith in Jesus, and they had done so because God had elected them. When other Cretans believed later on, the basic reason would be the same—God had elected them.

Probably Paul, as a pastor, would have encountered those who were troubled by the doctrine of election. Some of them might have preferred to see the Book of Life with their names recorded in it. Initially, that possibility might seem very attractive and helpful. But would it be? Andrew Bonar pointed out what the likely consequence would be: "If God were to reveal your election to you, you would believe in yourself instead of faith in Christ."[2] The faith of God's elect is faith in Jesus.

What, then, should our attitude be to the reality of divine election? Robert Murray McCheyne, a powerful preacher in Scotland in the third and fourth decades of the nineteenth century, also composed poems and hymns. In a verse of one of his hymns, he expressed his response to divine election, and his words are suitable for all believers:

> Chosen not for good in me,
> Wakened up from wrath to flee,
> Hidden in the Savior's side,
> By the Spirit sanctified;
> Teach me, Lord, on earth to show
> By my love, how much I owe.[3]

Our proper response to divine election is the same response that we should give to all God's blessings—gratitude and loving service. That is how Paul responded, and it is how all God's people should respond.

---

2. Andrew A. Bonar and Marjorie Bonar, *Reminiscences of Andrew A. Bonar* (London: Hodder and Stoughton, 1895), 140.

3. Robert M. McCheyne, "When This Passing World Is Done," in the public domain.

2

The Faith of God's People

TITUS 1:1b–2a

[1b]*The faith of God's elect and the acknowledgment of the truth which accords with godliness,* [2a]*in hope of eternal life.*

What is saving faith? How can we tell if our faith in Jesus is real? We know that there are verses in the Bible that describe temporary faith. Jesus said in His parable of the sower that there would be people who would follow for a time and then give up (Matt. 13:20–22). The reasons for giving up are different. Some give up because of troubles and opposition; others give up because of the pursuit of riches.

Jesus also stated in the parable that there would be differences between those who were true believers when He said that some would produce thirtyfold, others sixtyfold, and others a hundredfold (v. 23). We can imagine a person with thirtyfold standing beside a person with temporary faith, but at the time they are standing together the one with temporary faith seems to be making more progress because he is very enthusiastic and joyful. Eventually, however, it is the believer with thirtyfold who perseveres.

So it is important to understand the features of true faith. Faith in Jesus is the response to the gospel that makes the difference among those who hear it. Therefore, we can assume that certain marks will constitute what true faith is. Believers may not be aware of those features when they first believe, but as they continue to believe, they will discover them.

Exercise of Faith

Paul connects the faith of God's elect and their knowledge of the truth. When he speaks of "the truth" (Titus 1:1b), he has specific teaching in view. Perhaps he has in mind what Luke calls the "apostles' doctrine," in which the converts at Pentecost continued (Acts 2:42), or he may mean the truths that were contained in the gospel message that he and others declared. Whatever "the truth" refers to, it results in faith in Jesus.

For Paul, faith is not a vague notion that is based on empty ideas about mere possibilities. Instead, the faith that marks the ones he is describing is connected to their understanding of the truth that had been declared. When they heard the gospel about Jesus and His salvation, they were convinced inwardly about its accuracy and its relevance to them. Their confidence was the result of the inward working of the Holy Spirit.

In another of his letters, Paul describes what occurs when that takes place: "For our gospel did not come to you in word only, but also in power, and in the Holy Spirit and in much assurance, as you know what kind of men we were among you for your sake" (1 Thess. 1:5). Paul had preached the same gospel in Thessalonica as he had wherever he went, but he did not always have the same response as far as numbers were concerned. But whatever the numbers, the Holy Spirit had given to the converts a deep conviction about the truth of the message they had heard.

Often, a conviction of the truth of the gospel shows itself by listeners having a desire to admit their sinfulness. Everyone is sinful, but not everyone realizes it. All people will admit that they are imperfect, but through the message of the truth, they discover that such imperfections are serious and they are under divine judgment. Yet this discovery does not lead to despair and a sense of pointlessness. Instead, the gospel encourages them to repent, to confess their sins to the God they have offended. They find themselves drawn to do so and to ask God to forgive them. This consciousness of sin will vary among those who repent, but they will repent of their inward and outward sins.

Faith and repentance are often said to be like twins. Repentance is not saving faith, but it does accompany such faith. The faith that embraces Jesus is aware that He died for sinners. Indeed, thinking about Jesus on the cross stimulates both faith and repentance as the individual ponders who Jesus is and why He died. Faith turns a person to Jesus, but it does so from a penitent heart.

Sometimes when people are seeking to understand what is meant by responding to the gospel, they will be helped by reading what others have written about it. When I first read Spurgeon's book *All of Grace*, his explanation of what faith is helped me, although his explanation is not unique to him. He said that faith in Jesus is made up of three things: knowledge, belief, and trust. We need to be informed about Jesus, and the information is found in the Bible; we need to believe that the information is true; and we must then trust in Jesus.

So faith is marked by dependence on Jesus; that is to say, the sinner trusts in Him, especially on the basis of many biblical promises connected to forgiveness and pardon. There are different pictures of faith in the Gospels. Sometimes Jesus told sinners to come to Him, at other times He told them to look to Him, and at other times He told them to feed on Him. Those illustrations describe contact with Him.

We can see that faith in Jesus is a supernatural work of God in the inner lives of believers. It expresses itself in dependence on Jesus. Such faith is exercised by those who have been taught by the Holy Spirit that they are sinful and who have discovered through His guidance that Jesus is the only Savior.

Effects of Faith

Paul reminds Titus that while such faith itself is invisible, there is clear evidence of its existence, and that evidence is godliness. Those who believe in Jesus will commence to live transformed lives. This change occurs whenever conversions take place. It is the usual consequence, although as we noticed already, there will be degrees of change or fruitfulness in those who believe.

Another word for godliness is "sanctification," in which a believer dies to sin and lives to God. Sanctification is a lifelong process and never brings perfection in this life. Nevertheless, the Bible describes it as Christlikeness, which is a very positive way of describing holiness. Often, the concept of holiness is perceived as drab and dreary, yet the idea of Christlikeness informs us that holiness is actually a lifestyle of great beauty.

Holiness occurs because the believer is united to Jesus. In one of His parables, Jesus likened the relationship between Him and His people to that of a vine and its branches (John 15:1–17). The branches bear fruit because they are united to the vine. In the same way, Christians bear fruit through the life that comes to them from their union with Jesus. This life is the Holy Spirit working within them. Holiness, therefore, is not an attempt to attach something external to our faith, as if a gardener could use glue or a piece of string to attach fruit to a branch. Rather, holiness shows itself in the life of a person who is occupied with God and His salvation, who meditates on the Bible, who focuses on Jesus, who prays, who hates sin, and who desires to grow in grace. In other words, that person is experiencing ongoing inner renewal by the indwelling Spirit.

This does not mean that achieving holiness will be easy for Christians. They have three powerful enemies that will constantly aim to hinder their spiritual growth: the world, the flesh, and the devil. The *world* does not mean people, but the ideas, aims, and interests of fallen humanity; the *flesh* is the remaining desires for sin that exist in every believer; and the *devil* is the tempter, whose aim, among other things, is to get believers to sin against God.

God could have prevented this spiritual conflict, but He has not. Instead, He has provided His people with various helps to use in order to be holy. Because He has regenerated His people, they are now alive to Him and aware that they need His help. The devil will try to get believers to forget or to ignore the helps that the Lord has provided. Paul reminded other Christians that they had the responsibility to work out what the Lord had worked in them (Phil. 2:12–13). The Holy Spirit, who is in every believer, will enable all of them to grow in grace. Yet although they know that is the case, they can fail to appropriate the helps that are at their disposal.

What are those helps that God has provided for our holiness? One is the Bible. The best way for us to see how we look is to use a mirror. It will tell us if our hair is combed or if our tie is straight. In a spiritual sense, we have a mirror, God's Word. Meditating on it will reveal to us what we look like spiritually. The stories told in it will warn us about the dangers we face, as well as how others have responded to them. As someone said, sin will keep us from the Word, or the Word will keep us from sin.

A second help is prayer. Jesus teaches us in the Lord's Prayer that we must pray not to be led into temptation. It is possible to analyze the statement and forget to do what it says. Many of the psalms are about how the authors dealt with sin in their lives. We can ask the Lord to search our hearts (Ps. 139:23–24). We can ask the Lord to protect us from secret and presumptuous sins (19:12–13). We can imitate the psalmist who determined to hide God's word in his heart so that he would not sin against God (119:11). Prayer is important for walking in the way of holiness.

A third help is fellowship. Believers in Jesus are heading toward the same destination. They help one another on the way. We can ask other Christians to challenge us if they see us growing cold. Or we can encourage them by speaking of the things of God when we meet together. There are many ways by which we can do this, but one of the most important is attending church services regularly.

One of the concerns that Titus would have had is whether the converts in Crete would live holy lives. When we read the letter, we see easily that holy living is one of the matters that Paul raises repeatedly as he explains to Titus his responsibility to teach the different types of people connected to the churches there. Whether they were old or young, male or female, elders or not, they all had to be holy.

Holiness and Hope

Paul also says that God's holy people are looking ahead to their future experience, which he describes as the "hope of eternal life" (Titus 1:2a). We use the word "hope" often, but not always with the biblical use in mind. Sometimes we say, "I hope to go on vacation this year, but I might not be able to do so." When we use the word in that way, we are referring to something that is possible, even likely, but uncertain. In contrast to such a possibility, the New Testament describes the second coming of Jesus as the hope of His people, and while none of them know when it will occur, they are sure that it will happen. And when the word is used in this way, it also includes everything connected to salvation that will occur when He returns.

The particular aspect of the hope that Paul mentions here is eternal life. He does not mean that the experience of eternal life will commence when Jesus returns. Christians have eternal life from the moment they trust in Jesus. When Christians die and go to heaven, they still possess eternal life, even though they no longer have their body. But when Jesus returns, the resurrection will take place, and the Christians who have been in heaven will be reunited with their bodies, and they will then be perfect in soul and body. Believers who are alive on earth when Jesus returns will be perfected inwardly and outwardly. At that time, all believers will be able to experience eternal life in a manner that they could not do so previously.

In order to appreciate this aspect of hope, we have to grasp what eternal life is. Jesus explained what eternal life is when He said in His prayer in John 17:3 that "this is eternal life, that they may know You, the only true God, and Jesus Christ whom You have sent." Eternal life is much more than existing forever. It is about knowing experientially the Father and the Son through the work of the Holy Spirit.

While it is impossible for us now to explain what that experience will be like, we can see from various biblical passages that it will involve the companionship of Jesus (Revelation 7:17 reveals that one of the features of heaven is that Jesus leads His innumerable followers to "fountains of waters") and discoveries of the resources of God (as Paul says in Ephesians 2:7, God's people will be shown by the Father "the exceeding riches of His grace in His kindness toward us in Christ Jesus"), and the Holy Spirit will continually come from the throne of God and of the Lamb to supply the residents of the heavenly city with divine provision (Rev. 22:1).

These descriptions of the heavenly experience should whet our appetite for spiritual things. They are aspects of the hope of eternal life that should fill our vision of the future. Yet we know, sadly, that often this hope is not as strong as it should be. Why is that the case? Sometimes, it may be clouded by adverse experiences, although we are aware of people whose hope burned stronger during times of ill health and other disappointments. Sadly, the main cause of a dimmer hope is failure to progress in holiness. It is obvious from this verse in Titus that Paul connects holiness and hope; indeed, he says that hope is part of holiness. Dabbling with sin takes the eyes of our souls off our heavenly destination. The obvious response, if that is where we are (and who of us is where we should be?), is to repent of our folly and ask the God of all grace to restore us to a spiritual state in which we look ahead with hope to the world to come.

3

Who Is Our God?

TITUS 1:2b–3

[2b]*God, who cannot lie, promised before time began,* [3]*but has in due time manifested His word through preaching, which was committed to me according to the commandment of God our Savior.*

Years ago, when laptops and tablets and smartphones were new, I would make my way to the local bookstore to see what books could explain to me how these technologies worked and what I could do with them. Each time I went, I saw shelves full of books of different sizes; some were quite short, obviously designed for ignoramuses like me, and others were much longer and clearly meant for experts, or at least for those who wanted to become experts. Something similar can happen on shelves full of books on theology. We need books for those who know a little and books for those who know much more.

What can we say when we come to speak about God? After all, when we use the name God, we are saying everything about Him, even though we don't know everything about Him. When we say, "O God, help me!" in prayer at a time when we are desperate, we are aware that He possesses omnipotence, omniscience, wisdom, and many other divine abilities to deal with our circumstances, yet we do not express those attributes in detail. But there are times when merely using a divine name is not enough. In order to say something about Him that others can respond to, we need to say specific things about Him, truths that are suitable to the situation.

Paul does that here at the beginning of his letter to Titus as he describes his own calling.

Four Truths about God

In these verses of his greeting, Paul is reminding Titus of who their God is. He does not say everything he could have said about the Lord, but what he does say is connected to the situation he and Titus are in. Four details can be highlighted.

God Is Eternal

There are different ways of showing that God existed before time began. For example, we can see that He existed before He created the universe; if He did not exist before it, He could not have created it. Even a child recognizes that must be the case. In this verse Paul mentions that before time began, God promised eternal life would be given to His elect. Since no one else existed then, He must have promised within Himself. The reality of making this promise points to the doctrine of the Trinity and the covenant of redemption made by the persons of the Trinity, in which they engaged to save those who had been chosen by the Father, redeemed by the Son, and regenerated by the Spirit. The God we serve has no beginning; He is eternal.

God Is Truthful

Paul says of God that He "cannot lie" (Titus 1:2). He is completely truthful. In this regard, He is the opposite of the Cretans, whom Paul says later in this letter "are always liars" (v. 12), quoting one of their own prophets. We can see why God's truthfulness is important when we think about His eternal promise. If God told one lie, then how could He be trusted? Or He could decide not to keep His promise. But such a thought is blasphemy, an attack on the nature of God. As Spurgeon commented, "God is too great to need the lie and too good to wish to do such a thing."[1]

1. Charles Haddon Spurgeon, "What God Cannot Do!," *Metropolitan*

God Is Sovereign

Paul further mentions that God chose the appropriate time for making known His eternal promise. The time for making the promise known began when the apostles were entrusted with preaching the truths connected to it. This does not mean that people before then did not hear about eternal life. Rather, with the coming of the Savior and following His death, resurrection, and ascension, there was a huge expansion in the number of people experiencing the fulfillment of God's promise to give eternal life to sinners. And apostles like Paul were the vanguard in doing so.

Although apostles, in the sense that Paul was one, no longer exist today, it is still the divinely chosen time for spreading the message connected to sinners discovering the experience of eternal life. It was very comforting for gospel preachers in the past to know that the period between the two comings of Jesus is the time when God will bring salvation to His elect, that it is the period He sovereignly chose to do this. And it is very encouraging for preachers today as well. It is the time of the ingathering of His people, and already it has lasted almost two thousand years.

God Is Savior

Paul also reminds Titus that both of them are in a special relationship with God. He is their Savior. In this brief description of God, Paul says a great deal. Paul was a Jew and Titus was a Gentile, yet both had been rescued by God, a reminder that the Lord was doing something incredible when He brought together in the church those who previously were very far apart. Titus would have to work among Jews in Crete who had become followers of Jesus, and he and they would have to acknowledge the commonality of their salvation.

Moreover, Paul, in using this name for God, stated that both he and Titus were sinners. Paul had been a very religious Jew, but through the working of divine grace in his heart, he had discovered

---

Tabernacle Pulpit, vol. 10, May 8, 1864, The Spurgeon Center, "Sermons," https://www.spurgeon.org/resource-library/sermons/what-god-cannot-do/#flipbook/.

that he needed a savior, the Savior who had appeared to him on the road to Damascus. While we do not know much about Titus's background before he became a Christian, we know that he was a sinner who needed a savior. Both Paul and Titus had come to appreciate and rejoice in the amazing truth that the eternal God who is in control of time was and is fulfilling His promise to give eternal life to those He has saved from their sins.

How do we react to Paul's description of God here? Do we find we are saying to ourselves and to others that this God is amazing? Are we astonished that although He is so great, His greatness is revealed in a majestic way through His saving activities for sinners like us? Does our heart burn with love to the God who is determined to fulfill His eternal promise about each of His people?

Four Aspects of Paul's Service

Paul also states his role in the outworking of God's promise to give eternal life to His chosen people. He highlights four features of his role.

First, Paul had been commanded to perform this role by God, and since it was a command, it means that Paul's response was one of obedience. Once when Paul was testifying before a court about his ministry, he told King Agrippa about his conversion on the road to Damascus and then said to the king that he "was not disobedient to the heavenly vision" (Acts 26:19). In order to show how this had occurred, Paul gave a summary of his ministry: he had "declared first to those in Damascus and in Jerusalem, and throughout all the region of Judea, and then to the Gentiles, that they should repent, turn to God, and do works befitting repentance" (v. 20). Paul was not sinless, but he realized that he was under the authority of God at all times.

It is easier to want to obey a God who is a Savior. Recognizing that salvation is His gift freely provided creates a sense of gratitude in the heart of the one who serves Him in whatever role He has assigned to that person. It would be safe to say that Paul would have served even if God had called him to do something else. But since God called him to be an apostle, he served in that way.

Second, Paul had a message that described what God had done in order that sinners would have eternal life. That message, or word, was the gospel. Paul reminded the Romans that he had been set apart for "the gospel of God" (Rom. 1:1). Later in that chapter, he said that he was not ashamed of the gospel because it is the power of God for salvation (v. 16). It is "the word of the truth" (Col. 1:5) that he had been given and had taken to Crete when he had gone there with Titus.

Third, Paul had mainly communicated this message by preaching it. Paul meant that he proclaimed the message as a herald. A "herald" was a person who declared clearly and loudly a message from his superior; his superior could be a ruler or a military leader or someone in authority. A herald could announce that a war had been declared or that peace had been achieved. He could declare that his king was about to visit a location and tell the inhabitants to prepare for his coming. The herald spoke with authority because he had been instructed what to say. He did not compose his own message, nor did he adjust the message he had been given. When he gave his message, he spoke in such a way that his audience heard what he said.

The difference between Paul and a mere herald of an earthly superior was that when he declared the message, the power of God was with him. The message might have seemed irrelevant or ridiculous to some, yet as far as those who were promised eternal life were concerned, the One described in the message also came in a powerful way with the message and brought them out of darkness into His light. This is why Paul knew the gospel would have results.

Fourth, Paul says he had been entrusted with the declaration of the message of the gospel. When he wrote these words, he had been proclaiming it for about thirty years. He was able to look back on those years of service and say that he had been faithful to his calling. Indeed, in the last letter he wrote, he describes his service and how he has remained faithful to the One who called him: "I have fought the good fight, I have finished the race, I have kept the faith. Finally, there is laid up for me the crown of righteousness, which the Lord, the righteous Judge, will give to me on that Day, and not to me only but also to all who have loved His appearing" (2 Tim. 4:7–8).

In Paul's brief description of his ministry, there is a reminder and a challenge to Titus as to how he would work for the Lord in Crete. Yet the challenge was not just for him. It comes to all who serve the Master, even though they are not apostles. While their service will never be perfect, it should be marked by grateful obedience to God, precision in communicating the message, clarity and boldness in declaration, and persistent faithfulness over the years of service, with an eye to the Master's commendation when they meet.

4

Greetings to Titus

TITUS 1:4

---

[4]To Titus, a true son in our common faith: Grace, mercy, and peace from God the Father and the Lord Jesus Christ our Savior.

It was a common practice for writers to include a greeting in a message, and Paul and the other New Testament writers often include greetings addressed to the recipients of their letters. Greetings would include a description of the recipient as well as a statement wishing them well.

Paul's Description of Titus

Clearly there was a strong bond between Paul and Titus, and probably it began when Titus was converted through Paul's ministry. Although no details are given about Titus's conversion experience, Paul's calling him his true child suggests that Titus was a convert of Paul.

The description also indicates that there was an ongoing relationship between Paul and Titus, like that between a father and son. Today we would call it training and mentoring. Through the grace of God, Titus became like his spiritual father, Paul. By spending time with Paul, watching him in all kinds of situations, and listening to him as he preached, dialogued, and discussed the doctrines of the faith with others, Titus was helped to become the effective Christian leader he was.

It was not just with Titus that Paul had this type of relationship. Another biblical character who was involved with Paul in this way was Timothy (1 Tim. 1:2), and he too had been converted through Paul and then trained by him as a Christian leader. It is likely that other Christians Paul mentions, such as Tychicus, had a similar relationship with him.

We can easily see that Titus was a blessing to the churches with whom he interacted. But we must also note how he became such a blessing, and crucial to the process was Paul's training. Now Paul is drawing near to the end of his life, and it is a great comfort to him that he can have confidence in leaders such as Titus to carry on the work into the future.

Titus became the kind of leader Paul wanted; he was a true child as they served together in spreading the gospel. As we look at his character, we can see that he was a different kind of person from Timothy. The latter seems to have been weaker physically and possessed a timider character. Recognizing this is a reminder that the Lord uses very different people in His service, and Paul was aware of this as well. Even though Titus was a stronger person naturally than Timothy, they both needed divine resources, and Paul now reminds Titus of what he could and would receive from God on a continual basis.

Grace and Peace

In his greeting, Paul combines the common Gentile and Jewish greetings. Gentile writers used a similar word for grace when they were sending greetings to another person or group; Jewish people used the word for peace (shalom) when sending their greetings. Probably Titus would have been familiar with this Pauline greeting because it is unlikely that the apostle used it only when he was writing a letter. And we can imagine Titus thinking each time he heard the combined greeting that it depicted in a very moving and precious way the unity that the gospel had brought about between Jews and Gentiles. After all, Titus was a Greek, and Paul was a Jew. Now they shared the blessings of the Lord.

It is important to remember that the gospel breaks down barriers in every century and in every country and community where it comes. In the Western world today, society is very polarized, and sadly, churches can reflect those divisions, whether they are caused by race, wealth, status, or age. Other societies have their divisions. In the first century, Crete had them as well, and one effect of the gospel would be to create communities (churches) where such divisions would disappear and where true unity would occur.

What can we say about God's grace? One answer would be to ask, How many pages do we have? After all, the grace of God is so rich and varied that countless volumes could be written about it. So all we can do here is remind ourselves of some aspects of it.

The grace that God would give to Titus would always be *sufficient* for every situation he would face in Crete. This was the assurance that the Lord had given to Paul when he had to cope with the thorn in the flesh that He had allowed to afflict him (2 Cor. 12:8–9). So Paul was writing out of personal experience of the Lord's care. Obviously, this reality should be a means of great comfort to every believer. To know that God will never leave us short of necessary grace is very consoling and calming. And it would have been for Titus as he got on with the work assigned to him in Crete.

Further, the grace that God will give is always *sovereign* grace. By "sovereign" I mean that it is enabling grace that would equip Titus to make progress in each situation he would face. God's grace is more than His attitude toward unworthy sinners; it is also the expression of His power on behalf of unworthy servants. The Lord's grace is His power in action in a loving way. Maybe Titus looked at the Cretans and thought, *Which of these can be elders*? The answer is, those whom sovereign grace would develop into suitable people. We cannot forget, any more than Titus could, that sovereign grace achieves its intentions.

Furthermore, this divine grace *is usually given in answer to prayer*. This does not mean that God is not sovereign; instead, it means that He has, as the Sovereign, decreed the way for grace to be obtained. And the way that He has decreed shows the simplicity of receiving divine grace; we receive it when we ask for it. After all, that is what Paul is doing here; he is asking the Father to give necessary grace to one of His children who has an important role to fulfill in His service. One of the best-known verses in the Bible reminds us of this: "Let us therefore come boldly to the throne of grace, that we may obtain mercy and find grace to help in time of need" (Heb. 4:16). Paul prays that Titus would experience divine grace.

Titus could also experience peace from God as he served in Crete. In a sense, peace is only one aspect of grace. Yet it is an aspect that the Bible often highlights, which means that it is a blessing the Lord loves to bestow on His people again and again. Just as grace will always be sufficient for every situation Titus will face, so there will be peace that is suitable for every situation. Titus could know peace in even the most difficult of circumstances when everything seems to be working against him.

It may be that Paul is saying here that in addition to the Father and the Lord Jesus Christ being the divine suppliers of grace, they also provide distinct aspects of grace. This would mean that the Father provides grace suitable to Him being the Father of His family and the Son provides grace suitable to Him as the Savior of His church. There is great truth here, even if we think about only the differences the humanity of Jesus gives to His displays of affection and sympathy. Whatever distinctions there are between the supply of the Father and the supply of the Son, Paul's words indicate that they can be received simultaneously as well as abundantly.

We can observe that Paul immediately reminds Titus that no human leader has the necessary resources within himself to help the church to grow. Paul had many natural and spiritual gifts, yet he could not be the answer to the situations he faced. Similarly, Titus had many gifts, yet in himself he did not have the answer to the problems and difficulties he would face in Crete. Instead, he would have to depend on what he would receive regularly from the Father and the Son.

So Paul's greeting was full of encouragement for Titus. And Titus would need it, as Paul now reminds him of some of the tasks he must perform in Crete, beginning with the appointment of elders.

5

Importance of Elders

TITUS 1:5–16

5For this reason I left you in Crete, that you should set in order
the things that are lacking, and appoint elders in every city as I
commanded you—6if a man is blameless, the husband of one wife,
having faithful children not accused of dissipation or insubordina-
tion. 7For a bishop must be blameless, as a steward of God, not
self-willed, not quick-tempered, not given to wine, not violent, not
greedy for money, 8but hospitable, a lover of what is good, sober-
minded, just, holy, self-controlled, 9holding fast the faithful word as
he has been taught, that he may be able, by sound doctrine, both to
exhort and convict those who contradict.

10For there are many insubordinate, both idle talkers and deceiv-
ers, especially those of the circumcision, 11whose mouths must be
stopped, who subvert whole households, teaching things which they
ought not, for the sake of dishonest gain. 12One of them, a prophet
of their own, said, "Cretans are always liars, evil beasts, lazy glut-
tons." 13This testimony is true. Therefore rebuke them sharply, that
they may be sound in the faith, 14not giving heed to Jewish fables
and commandments of men who turn from the truth. 15To the pure
all things are pure, but to those who are defiled and unbelieving
nothing is pure; but even their mind and conscience are defiled.

16They profess to know God, but in works they deny Him, being
abominable, disobedient, and disqualified for every good work.

Paul's requirement of arranging for a group of elders in each congregation in Crete shows that competent elders are an essential feature of healthy churches. In Crete, they would help deal with the false teachers Paul mentions as well as guide the church through its future circumstances, which is what elders are intended to do in all churches.[1]

The term "elder" points to an individual's dignity that comes with experience and maturity. "Bishop" or "overseer" describes the task of the elder, which is to rule, and he does so according to the requirements of God's Word. In saying that an elder is "a steward of God" (Titus 1:7), Paul affirms that the church is a divine household with a God-appointed structure. Because elders have a divine Master, those called to the office should serve Him with reverence, love, and diligence.

Since appointing elders is the first matter that Paul mentions, we see the necessity of having pastors and other elders as effective leaders of local congregations. Paul's concern about elders can be divided into three areas, each of which has several applications. All of his applications here are connected to his concern about the importance of elders for counteracting the influence of false teachers in those congregations.

The Elder and His Local Witness

The first detail to note about elders is their *plurality*. Titus was not to appoint just one elder in a congregation. The reasons for this requirement probably were to prevent an abuse of power, to provide collective wisdom, and to ensure shared roles.

The second detail is that elders should be *local men* who lived in their towns. It is likely that the presence of recognized elders would give credibility to a congregation in the eyes of its community and perhaps even in the eyes of the civil authorities, who might be suspicious of a new set of meetings taking place in their area.

---

1. Scholars debate where the idea of elders came from. The most reasonable explanation is that the New Testament church continued the practice of the synagogue of having a group of mature men who were responsible for running its affairs. Probably similar arrangements took place within Gentile societies. It is likely that former synagogue elders in Crete, after they had become believers, would be useful church elders.

Paul's next comment, that an elder had to be *blameless*, indicates that the individual was known in his community for his character. Others in the location could look at the church and deduce that it was not a threat to civil order because of the character of its leaders. This would not guarantee the removal of opposition or persecution, but the presence of suitable local elders is essential for the good witness of a congregation.

But what does it mean to be blameless? Paul connects this requirement first to the elder's home and then to his character and practice. First, verse 6 says that an elder must be "the husband of one wife,"[2] which indicates that an elder must be male, and also "having faithful children not accused of dissipation or insubordination." Paul stresses that a person's home life matters, and if things are wrong there, he should not be an elder.

Paul makes clear to Titus what he requires when he says that the man's children should not be guilty of wild behavior and disrespect. This instruction reveals that unruly children were a problem at that time as well as at other periods in history. Describing them as children indicates that Paul does not have adult sons and daughters in mind (such would normally be married in any case).

Matthew Henry comments that "Children so faithful, and obedient, and temperate, will be a good sign of faithfulness and diligence in the parent who has so educated and instructed them; and, from his faithfulness in the less, there may be encouragement to commit to him the greater, the rule and government of the church of God."[3]

Paul will go on to specify in the letter how different persons connected to the church should behave, and some of them would

2. The requirement of "the husband of one wife" has been interpreted in various ways. Some scholars say that it prohibits polygamy. Others, including early church leaders and authors, say that Paul forbids eldership to a widower who has remarried. A third possibility is that Paul forbids an unmarried man from becoming an elder.

3. Matthew Henry, *Commentary on Acts through Revelation*, vol. 6 of *Commentary on the Whole Bible* (New York: Fleming H. Revell, 1959), 857.

be elders, some the wives of elders, and some children of elders. What Paul is concerned about as he describes elders is the witness of the elder and his family in the community, and he is saying that an elder should be known as a person who controls his family in a loving manner.

The Elder and His Christian Lifestyle

Paul then lists eleven features—five negatives and six positives—that explain what it means for an elder to be blameless or above reproach. The negative aspects are ugly, and the positive ones are beautiful. I don't think Paul is saying that once an elder is in office, he somehow becomes prone to those negative tendencies. Instead, Paul is saying that a person who already possesses them should not become an elder.

Some of the five negatives are not easy to see at times. Drunkenness or violence is easy to see, and quick-temperedness usually shows itself, but being self-willed and having greed for gain can be hidden from those who do not know well the people who have these character flaws (the idea behind the word translated "self-willed" could also mean "domineering," which is the opposite of humble leadership). So it would seem that Titus should not allow as an elder a person whom he does not know well.

In contrast to such ugly features, an elder must be "hospitable, a lover of what is good, sober-minded, just, holy, self-controlled" (v. 8). Again, Paul is not saying that an elder becomes that after he is chosen. Instead, he is to be selected because that is the kind of life he is already living. Such a man is hospitable, which means that he will open his home to Christians whom he can help. At that time, hospitality was often shown to Christians from other areas, especially because inns were not that common, and when they were available, they could be unsuitable for Christians to stay in. Hospitality could also be shown at local levels as well, such as in providing a place for Christian gatherings to occur.

A person who would be a suitable elder is one who loves "what is good" (v. 8). Such a description covers a wide range, whether concerning good people or good things. Calvin regarded it as meaning "devoted to kindness"; he contrasted it with the selfish traits that Paul has just forbidden.[4] While loving good probably means more than kindness, Calvin's insight highlights the importance of expressing in practical ways our appreciation of those who live in a good way.

Moreover, an elder will be "sober-minded" (v. 8), especially with regard to how he thinks. A church does not want as an elder someone who continually comes up with outlandish ideas. Instead, he is marked by thoughtful and sober reasoning about life and concerning how situations should be handled. Closely connected to this type of self-control is the possession of wisdom.

Three other features of an elder are mentioned, and they describe his conduct in different directions. He is just in his dealings with other people, holy in his relationship with God, and self-controlled (v. 8). Each of these features is intertwined and cannot be practiced apart from the others. It is impossible for a person to walk with God and live a disciplined life if he is not upright with his neighbors.

As mentioned earlier, Paul uses the illustration of a chief servant in a household when referring to elders. The steward's role was to see that other servants in the household did what the master wanted. He would ensure that servants in the kitchen and those in the garden worked together for the master. Therefore, he had to be on hand to encourage and guide the servants. This is a beautiful picture of an elder. He is a servant who helps other servants fulfill their roles. And in what way can he do this?

The Elder and His Task

Paul mentions only one task for the elder, and it is connected to communicating the "faithful word as he has been taught," presumably by Paul and Titus. The apostle mentions the commitment of an elder, revealed in his "holding fast" to the faithful word and not departing

4. John Calvin, *Commentaries on the Epistles to Timothy, Titus, and Philemon*, trans. William Pringle (Grand Rapids: Baker, 1998), 295.

from it. Clearly Paul's focus here is on teaching elders, although all elders should adhere to what God's Word says. "Holding fast" is a reminder of the importance of their having that message with them at all times, such as when giving counsel, and the reason they were to do so is because it alone is trustworthy. Obviously, the details of the trustworthy word are now found in the Bible.

There are two situations, says Paul, in which the teaching elder will use his knowledge, and they are very different. One is situations in which instruction is given, and the other is situations in which rebuke is called for. Christians need instruction in biblical doctrine, and it is the responsibility of teaching elders to provide it. At times Christians will need to be protected from distorters of the gospel, and it is the responsibility of teaching elders to rebuke those who are wrong. The information necessary for performing both responsibilities is found in Scripture, so we can see why elders should be holding it firm as they move through life. In a real sense, the church depends on them.

An obvious question that arises from this description of an elder and his work is how we apply it to a contemporary situation in which there is a plurality of elders in a congregation, of whom one or perhaps two will function as teacher or pastor, with the others being ruling elders.[5] First, the same lifestyle and heart disposition are required of both teaching and ruling elders, so the qualities Paul mentions are those expected today. Second, while God has endowed pastors with the special gift of teaching the church, this does not mean that ruling elders should be unable to teach the faith at other levels in the church, such as in Bible study groups or adult Sunday schools. All elders should be able to explain the faith and correct those who are mistaken and also be ready to rebuke those who persist in spreading wrong ideas and practices.

---

5. The differences between teaching and ruling elders have been discussed in various books on church government and order. For example, see John MacPherson, *Presbyterianism* (Edinburgh: T&T Clark, n.d.), 37–89.

The Danger Facing the Church

Paul was concerned about the progress, the purity, and the preservation of the churches in Crete. Each of these were under threat from false teachers, especially from those he calls the "circumcision" (v. 10). Those false teachers were Jews who focused on Jewish myths and genealogies and probably tried to find secret messages in them. Their practice allowed them space to talk about unprofitable matters, but in reality their behavior was only an expression of rebellion against God.

The method adopted by the false teachers was to aim at influencing households, including those connected to the churches, with the goal of making financial gain. They had been accurately described centuries previously by a Cretan prophet[6] who said that Cretans were "liars, evil beasts, lazy gluttons" (v. 12), which is a terrible character description. Paul applies that description to the false teachers in verses 15 and 16: "To the pure all things are pure, but to those who are defiled and unbelieving nothing is pure; but even their mind and conscience are defiled. They profess to know God, but in works they deny Him, being abominable, disobedient, and disqualified for every good work." Inevitably, persons who listened to them were led astray.

Paul instructs Titus to confront those false teachers in a manner that would make clear the seriousness of their devious behavior. It would not have been sufficient to ignore them and hope that their false teaching would somehow diminish and not affect the churches in Crete. The danger was real and threatening, and Titus had to be an example to the elders regarding how to defend the churches from such doctrinal dangers. Nevertheless, the rebuking had to have a right motive, which was that it had to be done with the aim of recovering the false teachers and those they had influenced to the right understanding of the faith.

---

6. Several early church leaders identified the Cretan prophet as Epimenides of Knossos, who lived in the sixth century BC.

It is unlikely that we will face the same false teaching today as Titus encountered in Crete. Nevertheless, there are many false teachers and members in churches who spread false ideas, despite their churches disapproving of them, who need to be rebuked in a firm and robust manner; otherwise, they will have an evil influence through a variety of means. If it was straightforward for the Cretan false teachers to access households, it is much easier for contemporary false teachers to do so through literature and other forms of media. So the leaders of each congregation need to be alert for such intrusions because they are a form of attack instigated by the devil.

6

Teaching Sound Doctrine

TITUS 2:1–6

---

[1]*But as for you, speak the things which are proper for sound doc-*
trine: [2]*that the older men be sober, reverent, temperate, sound in*
faith, in love, in patience; [3]*the older women likewise, that they*
be reverent in behavior, not slanderers, not given to much wine,
teachers of good things—[4]*that they admonish the young women*
to love their husbands, to love their children, [5]*to be discreet, chaste,*
homemakers, good, obedient to their own husbands, that the word
of God may not be blasphemed.
[6]*Likewise, exhort the young men to be sober-minded.*

Who should teach sound doctrine? Obviously, Titus was to do so, as we can see from Titus 2:1: "But as for you, speak the things which are proper for sound doctrine." Yet he was not the only one to do so. In the previous chapter, in verse 9, Paul says that elders are to teach sound doctrine: "Holding fast the faithful word as he has been taught, that he may be able, by sound doctrine, both to exhort and convict those who contradict." Titus was to be the role model for the Cretan elders regarding how to teach sound doctrine (vv. 7–8).

To whom should they teach sound doctrine? They should teach it to each group in the church. Paul mentions older men, older women, young women, young men, and bondservants. Teaching sound doctrine is necessary for their sanctification, their life of holiness. We can see that what Paul has in mind for teaching to each of these groups is very practical, concerned with their way of life.

Why should they teach sound doctrine? One answer is that inevitably there will be some form of teaching, and in Crete, rather than sound doctrine, it had been the pointless myths of the false teachers Paul mentioned in Titus 1. Today, there are many alternatives to sound doctrine, and the best way to combat them is by sound doctrine.

Older Men

Paul mentions six features that should mark the older men in the congregations in Crete. Each of them is essential, and none can be regarded as less important than the others. The first one is soberness. The idea is connected to being temperate, but its emphasis here is on being temperate in how a person thinks rather than in how he uses his body (usually a person is intemperate with his body because he is intemperate in how he thinks). Another possible translation is "clearheaded."

Paul repeatedly instructed believers regarding their thinking. A famous passage is found in Philippians 2:5–11, in which he tells the believers to think as Jesus did regarding status. Also in that letter, he reminds them that there is a direct connection between their thinking and their enjoyment of the presence of God (4:8–9). We can go through the Bible and discover many exhortations to right thinking and the spiritual benefits that it brings.

The second feature to be observed in an older Christian man is reverence. Paul is saying that such a person should not be childish. Instead, he behaves in a wise and appropriate manner that gains the admiration of others. He never behaves like a fool in any situation and earns respect from those who know him. We have all known men who behaved in this way, who stood out from others.

The third element of a Christian older man is being "temperate," or marked by self-control. This does not merely mean that he does not lose his temper when provoked. Nor does it mean that he puts a smile on his face but inside is simmering like a kettle about to spout out its heated water. Rather, it means that he is in control of all that he does. He is self-controlled when he buys a house or a car, when he speaks about another person, when he finds himself in prosperity or in poverty, when he assesses a situation, and when he is well or unwell.

A person marked by self-control will be calm and peaceful. I like the story of a Scottish Christian who was on a ship caught in a severe storm. The passengers began to panic, but he sat through the storm calmly. In fact, he was so peaceful that the panic-stricken passengers thought he was not even praying. He replied to them that he pitied those who had only begun to pray when the storm came. There is a sense in which believers are self-controlled because they know that God is in control.

The fourth feature of a Christian older man is that he should be "sound in faith." How does faith express itself when exercised by an older man? After all, such a person usually has the benefit of years of Christian experience. He will therefore be able to look back and see how the hand of God has guided and helped him through a variety of circumstances. Therefore, his faith will be marked by gratitude to God and by confidence that the God who helped in the past will do so in the future. His experiences will have taught him that the simpler his faith is, the better for his spiritual comfort.

Yet it is possible that some of the older men to whom Paul was referring might not have been Christians for a long time. They may have been converts from his recent visit to the island. Does an older man who is a recent convert need a certain emphasis in his faith that might not be present to such a degree in the faith of a younger believer? After all, both the older and the younger person believe in Jesus for salvation. Common sense should tell an older believer that he has fewer years left in this life, and therefore he should be focusing on what God will do for him in Christ during that period and when it is over. His faith should lead him to pray for grace for each day and for preparation for the next world.

Alongside faith, the older Christian man will be marked by "love," the fifth feature. Paul does not specify if he means love for God or love for other Christians or love for all people. But then he does not have to distinguish between them because these loves always exist together. If love for God is strong in a person's heart, then he will love God's people and those who need His saving grace. Paul is saying here that an older Christian man should be a living example of what is written in 1 Corinthians 13. Love makes him into a practical believer, full of compassion.

The sixth feature of an older Christian man is "patience," which is the determination to hold on to what is right even when the going is tough or mundane. It also contains what some have described as "stickability," that he will always be there, will be reliable. The basic requirements for such patience or endurance are loyalty, consistency, and devotion, and it is not difficult to see how they are connected to faith and love.

Looking at these six details reminds readers that Paul is calling his older male readers to function as patterns for younger men to imitate. When they have these features, the older men become credible role models. The presence of such features is also proof that the older men are aiming at Christlikeness because, after all, Jesus is the perfect example of a person with those features. Yet it is also important to remember that Paul is not demanding perfection; instead, he is looking for progress in the Christian life from those who, age wise, are the older males in the churches in Crete. And through Paul's words, Jesus calls all His older male followers to develop such beautiful and balanced lives.

Older and Younger Women

Paul also informs Timothy about the teaching of sound doctrine that is suitable for female Christians. We can understand how the family situations in society at that time were very different from what many are used to today. It was customary then for extended household groups to live together or to live close to one another. That may still happen today, but often it does not. Nevertheless, it is not that difficult to deduce principles from Paul's instruction that we can apply to our current circumstances.

Paul's words indicate he is describing older married women and their lifestyle in a situation in which they had regular contact with younger married women. It may have been normal for married older women in that society to provide direct guidance and example to younger women through close household contact, and if that was the case, Paul is saying that older Christian women should do so in a godly way. In order to be able to do so, they had to have three features in their lifestyle.

The first feature is "reverent in behavior" (v. 3), which should mark all they say and do. We can see what Paul means by "reverent" through his use of the word "likewise," which points back to what he has said about older men in the previous verse. Those men were to be "sober, reverent, temperate, sound in faith, in love, in patience" (v. 2). Reverence is also an attitude of the heart indicating devotion to God.

Without the older women having such reverence, there would be wrong motives in their words and actions, and Paul mentions two negative features incompatible with reverence. One is that they should be able to control their speech and not use abusive words about other people. The other is that they should not be controlled by any substance; here it is wine, and we can see how too much wine could lead to uncontrolled, unsuitable talk.

The type of teaching that Paul has in mind is training, which emphasizes that any instruction has to be modeled by the teacher over a period of time. It is not difficult for a teacher to say what another person should do, but if the teacher does not live out the teaching in daily life, the message he or she will give is that the teaching does not matter very much. The training here concerns life in the home.

We are used to the concept of lifelong learning, and Paul identifies areas in which women contribute to the life of the home as their children are growing up. It is not difficult to see how older women could help younger women when their children are infants or are older or are teenagers because they would have had experience in those situations. They needed to work with their husbands to develop a home in which children are brought up in Christian ways. That truly is a high calling, one to which God calls them because He regards it as of utmost importance.

In addition to highlighting the priority of loving their husbands and children, Paul mentions several characteristics that should mark younger women and be modeled for them by the older women. They are to be self-controlled—and how could an older woman who engaged in slander and was influenced by a substance like wine model such control? Paul refers to self-control or temperate living several times in this letter, and not just for women. His references indicate its importance for an authentic Christian lifestyle. Moreover, the young women's lives should also be marked by purity of character, diligence in the family, generosity to the needy, and acceptance of God-ordained authority in the home.

The reason for such training is to ensure that Christians make a high impression on others of the importance of the Word of God. Christians desire to give the message that they live according to the Bible, and it is not difficult for non-Christians to discover if that is the case.

It is obvious that much of what Paul says here about both older and younger women is very different from contemporary views of their roles. Many people today will regard his teaching as old-fashioned and outdated, and others may regard them as offensive and insulting. Yet for Christians, his words are not notions he devised himself but the divinely inspired words of God.

His instructions to Titus on this matter are a call to older and younger women to have appropriate mutual involvement in family life, a mutual appreciation of the need to share and receive mature wisdom and insight in order to bring about godly home life. The men in Christian churches have their responsibilities, but so do the women. The contribution demanded involves hard work and a willingness to share and learn. But the outcome, under the blessing of God, of holy families makes the effort worthwhile.

Young Men

From one perspective, Paul does not say a great deal about the young men in the Cretan congregations. Only one requirement is mentioned, that of being "sober-minded" (v. 6), although his use of the word "likewise" would remind them to take note of what he had said to the other age groups he mentioned. Nevertheless, his focus here on sobriety, or self-control, allows us to consider it in more depth.

Is Paul indicating that most problems would not arise in Cretan people's lives if they were marked by sobriety? Probably lack of self-control was one reason why the Cretans had developed a reputation as gluttons and liars. Paul has already stressed the importance of moderation in the lives of older men and women as well as in young women. So it is obvious that Paul regarded self-control to be a crucial aspect of and evidence for their ongoing sanctification as Christians living in a difficult society.

The mention of self-control may cause a problem for some Christians because it seems to suggest that they can do something themselves to bring about personal control of their own lives, followed by ongoing improvement. In response to this suggestion, we have to insist that self-control is a fruit of the Spirit, a characteristic He produces in the lives of all Christians alongside the other beautiful features Paul mentions in Galatians 5:22–23.[1]

At the same time, it is obvious from the term "self-control" that self is a source of some of the problems that Christians experience. This is a reminder that Christians are involved in an ongoing conflict in which their indwelling sin is at war with the Spirit. How does a Christian deal with indwelling sin? One essential way is through self-control by the power of the Spirit.

Proverbs 25:28 reminds us of the importance of self-control when it says that "a man without self-control is like a city broken into and left without walls" (ESV). Such a city is defenseless against attack from enemies. Spiritual enemies will easily defeat a person who is not self-controlled. Just as such a city could be entered from

1. There are two Greek terms usually translated as "self-control." The word in Titus 2:6 is connected to sound judgment, whereas the other word used, for example in the list mentioned in Galatians 5:22–23, has the idea of the inner strength that enables people to control themselves. Both ideas are in harmony with each other and don't suggest a contradiction. We need right thinking and strong resolve in order to have self-control.

a wide range of possible locations, so Christians without sobriety in their thinking are wide open in many areas of life for spiritual invasion and defeat.

How Does a Christian Become Self-Controlled?

Christians must remember that self-control will be expressed *individually*. Each person has his or her own temperament that can be very different from another person's. We can easily see how a short-tempered person normally needs self-control, but we may overlook the possibility that a more dispassionate person also needs self-control because, after all, that person is perhaps lacking in Christian love. So in order to have self-control, Christians must engage in self-examination in order to know who they are.

Further, Christians must engage in self-control *intentionally*. There is the danger that we assume we can be passive about it because self-control is a fruit of the Spirit. But that is not how the sanctification process works. Instead, God commands each person to become self-controlled. A passive response is not how one responds to a legitimate command. Instead, there must be an active, intentional desire and determination to be self-controlled.

Then, believers must engage in self-control *intelligently*. It is impossible to become self-controlled when bypassing one's intellect. Self-control is obviously connected to what right or wrong aspirations or behavior is, and therefore it cannot be achieved if we don't know what the essential elements of biblical self-control are. We have to be instructed by God in these matters, and He has provided the information in the Bible.

And we can say that a believer will practice self-control *indefinitely*. We can see that is the case from the way Paul in this chapter insists that self-control must be a feature of all-age discipleship. There will never be an hour in his or her conscious life in which a believer will not have to practice self-control.

A fifth detail in developing self-control is finding good examples to *imitate*. The obvious example is Jesus, and the four Gospels show us how He was always marked by self-control. But there are others, too, such as Joseph having self-control when tempted by the wife of Potiphar or David exercising self-control when he refrained from slaying his enemy Saul.

The final detail about how a Christian becomes self-controlled is to recall that Paul makes it clear believers can attain it. This should be very encouraging to us, especially if we have to wrestle frequently with difficulties in this area of Christian living. No matter how difficult we may find some of our attitudes to be, it is wonderful to know that self-control is still attainable.

Why Should a Young Man Exercise Self-Control?

There are several answers to this question. First, a failure to exercise self-control can have lasting consequences—one wrong action in his youth may hinder or prevent a young man from achieving things that would have been within his grasp. This can happen in many different ways.

Second, failure to exercise self-control will give sin a grip on his character that he may struggle to get rid of. He may start to indulge in a habit that will become part of his character, or he may engage in a secret sin that will enslave him in the sense that it will become a compulsion.

Third, he should want to live as obediently to God's commandments as he can. The psalmist asks this question in Psalm 119:9: "How can a young man cleanse his way? By taking heed according to Your word." A good model for young men is Daniel; because he obeyed God, he prospered.

Fourth, a Christian young man is supposed to be a good example to other young males. Often, those who are younger will look up to a young adult male and imitate him in the way he speaks, in the things he does, in the interests he has developed. A young man cannot forget that he is always having an influence, and he should want to have a good effect on others.

Fifth, a young Christian male will want to please Jesus. He will wish to be like the young men whom Jesus trained to be His disciples, who spent time with Him and listened to His teachings.

While he cannot listen to Jesus personally, he can learn His teachings through prayer and meditation on the Bible. And although he may not become a preacher, he will become Christlike.

Sixth, a young Christian man will want to avoid the mistakes that other young men have made because they did not exercise self-control. One such person was John Mark, who did not control his desire to return home early from a commitment he had made to help Paul and Barnabas (Acts 13:13). The consequence was that Paul lost confidence in Mark and could not trust him for a while. In God's grace, Mark repented of his failure and later became very useful in the Christian church, writing a gospel and serving alongside other leaders, including Paul. So there is encouragement for those who fail.

In What Areas Should a Person Exercise Self-Control?

A simple and correct answer to this question is, in every area. Nevertheless, the Bible identifies areas of life in which self-control is essential, whatever age a person is. The ones I will briefly mention can be misused differently by individuals according to their age, so it is important to be aware of them; otherwise, we may fail with regard to them.

James, the Lord's brother, highlights the importance of Christians controlling their tongue (James 3:1–11). Through a series of powerful illustrations, he shows the consequences of misusing the tongue. One does not have to tell a lie in order to deceive. Exaggeration regarding the truth can be as destructive as a straightforward untruth. Gossip has done untold harm. We should always ask ourselves if we need to say the words we are about to say.

A second aspect of life in which people must engage in self-control is in their thoughts. It is easy to let our thoughts drift all over the place. Paul makes it very clear in Philippians 4:8 that God's people should control their thoughts: "Finally, brethren, whatever things are true, whatever things are noble, whatever things are just, whatever things are pure, whatever things are lovely, whatever things are of good report, if there is any virtue and if there is anything praiseworthy—meditate on these things."

A third area in which we must practice self-control is in our use of time. Often people will say, "I don't have the time to do that," and they have not really worked out whether they can do it or not. Paul tells the Ephesians, "See then that you walk circumspectly, not as fools but as wise, redeeming the time, because the days are evil" (Eph. 5:15–16).

Self-control must also govern our use of our talents. Sometimes people's talents govern their life, and all they do is try to find a way to express them. The danger, then, is that they become selfish and uncaring regarding the needs of others. Sometimes people realize that a situation will be better if they do not insist on displaying their talents.

Self-control will also enable a Christian to deal with strong temptations. As with the other areas mentioned, self-control will be accompanied by prayer for the Lord's help and for a sense of His presence in order to overcome the tactics of the devil. Yet it is obvious that the most effective way of dealing with temptation is to say no.

Therefore, we can see from Paul's instructions about how older and younger men and women are to live that the quality of their lives should adorn the gospel and give credibility to its message. The way they live is the only way they can do this, and there will be negative consequences if they refuse to follow his instructions. God will be displeased, the world will be unimpressed, and the churches will be stifled in their spiritual growth.

7

The Teacher of Sound Doctrine

TITUS 2:7–8

---

[7]In all things showing yourself to be a pattern of good works; in doctrine showing integrity, reverence, incorruptibility, [8]sound speech that cannot be condemned, that one who is an opponent may be ashamed, having nothing evil to say of you.

Sometimes a person may be asked to engage in a challenging task. An employer may select a worker to start a new branch of a firm in another location. The person chosen to do this would regard the invitation as a privilege yet be aware of new responsibilities connected to the task. At the same time, the employee would recognize that the employer was aware of his gifts for the role, which would convey some sense to him that he is suited for it. We could even imagine that an employer would select a suitable person and send him to oversee the development of several projects in an area.

Something like that, but far more consequential, had happened to Titus. Paul had charged him to develop several new churches in Crete. We don't know how many, except that Paul says that one existed in every town in the island (Titus 1:5). The task Paul gave to Titus was to teach these new believers about how to live as Christians in their homes and in their churches and to avoid being influenced by alternative teachings that threatened the call to Christian living. Yet, as Matthew Henry pointed out, Titus "could not expect so successfully to teach others, if he did not conduct himself well both in his conversation and preaching."[1] By "conversation," Henry means "behavior."

There is probably an indication here that Titus himself was a young man, because Paul connects his words in verse 7 to what he had said in verse 6. Titus certainly was younger than Paul. If Titus were a young man, we can see why it would be important for him to be a model for other young men in the churches. He would need to remember that those especially among the membership of the churches would look to him as an example of how to live for Christ.

In order for Titus to succeed, Paul identifies three crucial factors for Titus's ministry in Crete. First, in his behavior Titus had to be a model of good works; second, he needed to teach with integrity, reverence, incorruptibility, and sound speech; and third, opponents should not be able to condemn him or the Christian church in general.

Model of Good Works

Almost by definition, a Christian preacher has a public presence. People will see what he is like and, in doing so, will see who he is. One crucial aspect of his message is that his lifestyle must be consistent with it. Paul makes clear that this consistency must affect every area of Titus's life because it must be seen "in all things" (Titus 2:7). There should not be an area of his life that is out of tune with his service for the Lord.

Jesus criticized the Pharisees for not practicing what they preached (Matt. 23:3). He told His disciples that they should listen when the Pharisees taught what was consistent with God's Word, but they should not imitate the Pharisees' inconsistency between their teaching and actions. Paul himself had been a Pharisee and would have been aware of the problem of inconsistency that marked them. We should not be surprised that Paul insisted on ongoing consistency in Titus's ministry.

---

1. Matthew Henry, *Commentary on Acts through Revelation*, vol. 6 of *Commentary on the Whole Bible* (New York: Fleming H. Revell, 1959), 863.

In what ways would Titus reveal that consistency? There were many aspects of his life to consider, and one of them is Paul's call for "good works" (Titus 2:7), which he mentions several times in this letter. By "good works" he does not mean only acts of charity, although it would have been appropriate for Titus to have participated in them. Rather, by "good works" Paul means holy actions, the opposite of bad works. Holy living is what makes a pastor consistent with his high calling.

I noted that Titus was probably a young man when he received the letter from Paul. Perhaps we might assume that such advice from Paul involving consecration of Titus's entire life was unrealistic for a young minister. Yet those words have not been regarded as unrealistic by other young pastors.

Robert Murray McCheyne (1813–1843), who died before he was thirty in the middle of what would be regarded as a very effective ministry, is known for the statement that "a holy minister is an awful weapon in the hands of God." He wrote those words in a letter to Daniel Edwards, a colleague in the ministry who was also a young man: "Remember you are God's sword,—His instrument,—I trust a chosen vessel unto Him to bear His name. In great measure, according to the purity of perfections of the instrument, will be the success. It is not great talents God blesses so much as great likeness to Jesus. A holy minister is an awful weapon in the hand of God."[2]

His Manner of Teaching

Paul has already described to Titus what the contents of his teaching should be as he considered the various groups of people who composed the churches in Crete. So the description he provides in Titus 2:7–8 when he refers to "integrity, reverence, incorruptibility, sound speech" focuses more on the manner of Titus's teaching than on its matter or content. That was the kind of teacher Titus was to be. Titus probably already knew that was the case, but the description

---

2. Andrew A. Bonar, *Memoir and Remains of the Rev. Robert Murray M'Cheyne* (1844; repr., Edinburgh: Banner of Truth, 1966), 282.

reveals to us the importance of preachers being reminded of *how* they should teach as well as *what* they should teach.

Paul urges Titus to show "integrity" in his teaching. "Integrity" includes "honesty" within its range of meaning. This means that a preacher or an elder is not to wear a mask as he teaches, pretending to be something that he is not. It would be straightforward for a preacher to use words in order to create an impression that he is great. But such attempts only hide Christ from the preacher's hearers.

There are many kinds of masks a preacher can wear. He can pretend that he is practicing the pattern of prayer that he recommends. He can pretend that he is a devout preparer of sermons when he is only repeating other people's thoughts, a practice that can be avoided by simply saying where the thoughts came from.

Teaching that is marked by integrity will also avoid manipulating listeners. It is not hard for a preacher to work out what kind of details in his sermons will affect his audience. If he knows that emotional stories will move them, he will use those stories to create an atmosphere. If he discovers that the congregation prefers certain types of sermons, he can focus on those in order to get his hearers to approve of him.

A third aspect of absence of integrity in preaching is when the preacher engages in man pleasing. While this way of doing things may be similar at times to manipulation, it can also be different in the sense that the preacher aims to please men rather than God. Usually, man pleasing occurs when the preacher is more concerned about the opinion of humans than about what God says in His Word. It can be caused by fear of men or by wanting the flattery of men. But it reveals a lack of integrity in the preacher.

The second characteristic that Paul requires in a preacher is "reverence." By "reverence" Paul has in mind the awareness that a preacher should have of the position he is in. He is standing between God and people as the messenger of Jesus Christ. As he stands there, he is declaring a message that is marked by solemn issues, and he must present his material in a manner that reveals his recognition of that. A preacher is not being reverent when he speaks in a manner unsuitable to his location as well as to his calling. He is at all times a representative of Jesus Christ.

The third characteristic mentioned by Paul is "incorruptibility." This refers to Titus's sincerity rather than to the message he would preach. He was not to be a deceiver of souls. Instead, he was to be an example of a true servant of the Lord, uninfluenced by wrong motives or misusing the position he had been given. His life was to be marked by inner godliness, a holy disposition.

The fourth characteristic that Paul mentions for the benefit of Titus is "sound speech that cannot be condemned." The word "sound" means "healthy or wholesome." It may be the case that Paul is disapproving of rhetorical techniques that would produce unhealthy effects for which listeners may find fault. Rather, the preacher is a representative of the Healer of souls, and his manner as well as his message should produce good outcomes. If a medical doctor did not speak clearly or to the point, she would be of no help to her patient. Similarly, a preacher or teacher presents his message with the aim of bringing health to his listeners.

One way we can see integrity, reverence, incorruptibility, and soundness of words illustrated is to consider the preachers approved of by God in the Bible. The Old Testament prophets and the New Testament apostles stood as agents of God before people, and we can see from their messages that they took their responsibilities seriously and communicated with care the messages that they had been charged with delivering. It is true that they were moved deeply when they preached, but their emotional expression suited the aspects of the message they were speaking about. They could weep when the message focused on dire consequences for their listeners, and they could rejoice when their message was concerned with the good things of salvation.

Another way of doing this is to reflect on the methods of Jesus when He preached. It is evident that He was not a preacher who pretended to be what He was not, who tried to manipulate people by what He said, or engaged in man pleasing as He preached. He spoke with great authority the message that the Father had given

Him to declare (John 12:49). His sermons were marked by plainness of speech and were intended to bring spiritual health to his listeners.

Paul's concern was that an opponent should have nothing evil to say about Titus or the churches in Crete (Titus 2:8). If they failed to live correctly, they would be condemned by opponents. Observe, as Calvin says, how opponents could use these failures: "Everything that they can seize on as improper in our conduct is maliciously turned against Christ and His doctrine. The consequence is, that, through our fault, the sacred name of God is exposed to insult." The lesson, as he points out, is obvious: "Accordingly, the more we perceive that we are keenly observed by enemies, let us be the more attentive to guard against their calumnies, and thus let their malignity strengthen in us the desire of doing well."[3]

---

3. John Calvin, *Commentaries on the Epistles to Timothy, Titus, and Philemon*, trans. William Pringle (Grand Rapids: Baker, 1998), 315.

8

Bondservants

TITUS 2:9–10

---

[9]Exhort bondservants to be obedient to their own masters, to be well pleasing in all things, not answering back, [10]not pilfering, but showing all good fidelity, that they may adorn the doctrine of God our Savior in all things.

Paul now deals briefly with a final group of people in the churches in Crete, those he describes as "bondservants" (the word translated "bondservants" is *doulous*, the plural of *doulos*, meaning "slaves"). They are not a new set of people because Paul would have referred to some of them, if not most, in the previous verses when he mentioned old men and old women, young women and young men. The main difference now is that he is referring to their role in society rather than their roles in the church.

The Existence of Slaves

Slavery was a fact of life in the ancient world, and it was possible that the majority of the members of a church would have been slaves. Some were born as slaves, whereas others became slaves through adverse circumstances such as having debt or being captured in war. Slavery affected all kinds of people whom we would not usually associate with slavery today. Lawyers and doctors and teachers could be slaves. Sometimes slaves could purchase or earn their freedom. It was also the case that a wealthy person could adopt a slave as his heir.

Probably slave owners imposed degrees of confinement and had degrees of trust with regard to their slaves. It would have also been the case that most slaves would want freedom, although what they would have understood by social freedom is different from what we include in that concept.

There were some benefits in being a slave. Usually the owner, especially for household slaves, would provide a place to stay, clothes to wear, and food to eat. In a society in which there were no social services, we can see why some people would prefer to be slaves, especially if the owner was kind. If the owner was indifferent or cruel, then his slaves would have had a hard and miserable life.

There were slave rebellions in the Roman Empire, but they were crushed with ferocity by the authorities. Given the influence Christianity had among slaves, we can understand why Paul would stress their careful submission to their masters in case the authorities concluded that Christianity could lead to further social disorder among slaves.

Yet what does slavery mean today? Are we in the West not profiting from virtual slavery in the sweatshops of the East, where clothes and other products are produced at exceptionally cheap rates in order to provide for our materialistic desires? It is quite a sobering experience to go through one's wardrobe, look at the labels indicating where the products were made, and ask oneself how much the individuals who made each item earned.

Paul was writing to people for whom slavery was a fact of life. His words reveal that he took real life seriously, and while he probably prayed for a time when slavery would be unknown, he also wanted Christians who were slaves to live in a way in which they could honor God in their circumstances and know His blessing on their lives in the present.

The Employment of Slaves

Paul's instructions indicate that the gospel, once believed, affects every area of life, including those areas where it might be more demanding to live for God. The apostle's instructions are designed to liberate the bondslave internally, even though he or she is enslaved externally. How can such persons know inner freedom? They could do so by voluntary submission (indicated by the middle voice of the verb) from the heart to those who were their earthly masters. Paul did not urge Christian slaves to have a sullen acceptance of what was demanded of them. He gives a general goal, which is that slaves are to be well pleasing to their masters, and then gives two negative practices and one positive attitude that should bring about the goal.

The two negative practices are answering back and pilfering. Answering back was a common response of slaves to their masters, whether clearly spoken or muttered. Yet it is also likely that Paul has in mind the way a Christian slave interacted with those who worked alongside him or her. It is not difficult for us to see how this applies in a workforce today. In such situations, there will be many arguments over a wide variety of matters, but Christians are not to get involved in them because they are distractions from their service of Christ.

The second negative practice that Paul forbids is pilfering. "Pilfering" is another word for stealing. No doubt slaves in Paul's day would have thought nothing of taking small items that belonged to their master, just as many employees think nothing of the practice today. John Calvin says that in ancient times the words "thief" and "servant" were interchangeable.[1] We are aware that pilfering costs large amounts of money today in workplaces.

Why does Paul highlight those two matters of arguing and pilfering? The answer is simple. A person who does them does not possess the positive attitude of "showing all good fidelity" (Titus 2:10). By "fidelity" is meant faithfulness toward the master, and wasting his time by arguing and stealing his possessions are not indicators of such faithfulness. This dedication to the master was to be visible to all (showing) and to be comprehensive in nature (slaves were not free to pick and choose what they wanted to obey).

---

1. John Calvin, *Commentaries on the Epistles to Timothy, Titus, and Philemon*, trans. William Pringle (Grand Rapids: Baker, 1998), 316.

Would Paul have had particular consequences in view in making this request of Christian slaves? I would suggest three possibilities. First, the way they worked was an important aspect of evangelism; if they served as best they could with God's help, the master would note the contrast with other slaves and wonder why there was a difference. In some cases, he would ask why they behaved in such a devoted manner, and then the slave would be able to speak about the Savior.

Second, the manner of their serving was part of their personal growth in sanctification. Most of the slave's time would be spent in the master's service, so it would be in those circumstances that slaves would have to work out their own salvation. Yet as Paul told the Philippians, each Christian, whether a slave or not, would be working out the grace that God was already providing for him or her (Phil. 2:12–13). After all, the primary reason the slave was serving the earthly master in all that was required was that he or she was already serving a heavenly Master who had called him or her to work there.

Third, the practice of faithful service to a master would be good evidence that a male slave was capable of holding office in the church. It is a mark of an overseer that he is able to govern his family well. Similarly, it was often the case that a gifted slave would be given special responsibilities by his master, and faithfulness in those roles would indicate that he could be trusted in the church, whereas unfaithfulness would indicate he could not. After all, Jesus did say that "he who is faithful in what is least is faithful also in much; and he who is unjust in what is least is unjust also in much. Therefore, if you have not been faithful in the unrighteous mammon, who will commit to your trust the true riches?" (Luke 16:10–11).

It is not difficult to see how those aspects are guidelines with regard to how a Christian does his or her work today. Employment is an area where Christians have to work out their own salvation, where evangelism can be a consequence of loyal service, and where meeting responsibilities effectively will reveal whether the person can be given responsibility in the church.

The Reason

As with his comments to the young women ("that the word of God may not be blasphemed" [Titus 2:5]) and to Titus ("that one who is an opponent may be ashamed, having nothing evil to say of you" [v. 8]), Paul gives his reason why Christian slaves should behave as he has indicated. The reason is that "they may adorn the doctrine of God our Savior in all things" (v. 10).

The apostle states clearly that the doctrine, or teaching, belongs to God. Which divine person is he referring to? In the next verse he refers to the Father, so that could indicate that he has the Father in mind in verse 10. Yet in verse 13, Paul calls Jesus by the titles of God and Savior, so it looks as if the apostle actually has Jesus in mind in the description of God in verse 10.

As Paul has pointed out, the doctrine belongs to God, but it also has practical effects in every area of life. This means two outcomes at least. First, it is wrong for a Christian to think that there are some areas of life in which biblical doctrine does not apply. Second, Christians need to know what the doctrine is so that they can apply it in all aspects of their lives. The biggest problem facing many Christians is not the complexity of a situation but their ignorance of the principles of God's Word. This would have been a problem for first-century slaves if they were not taught the instructions given by Jesus that He commanded His apostles to pass on to the church.

Paul also affirms here that the godly lives of Christian slaves could make the gospel look more attractive. The word translated as "adorn" was often used to describe jewelry that was worn on attractive clothes. The clothes were attractive in themselves, just as the doctrine of the gospel is attractive in itself. Yet even as jewelry drew attention to the attractive clothes, so godly living draws attention to the gospel.

Many of the slaves to whom Paul was referring would have spent a lot of time adorning their masters and their wives. Male slaves often helped the master wear his best attire, and female slaves did the same for the master's wife. They may have regarded as pointless the way the master and his wife dressed up for a few hours before taking off their adornments. In contrast, the real adorning of these slaves would be permanent and valuable in the sight of God. Paul's words are a challenge to Christians today regarding how they are adorning the gospel by their style of living.

9

The Difference That Grace Makes

TITUS 2:11–12

---

[11]*For the grace of God that brings salvation has appeared to all men,* [12]*teaching us that, denying ungodliness and worldly lusts, we should live soberly, righteously, and godly in the present age.*

In the previous section of his letter to Titus, Paul has given instructions to him about various groups in the church—old and young, male and female, and slaves. What is the main, overriding reason each group should live in the manner Paul mentions? He tells us in verse 11: "For the grace of God...has appeared."

The Grace of God

The grace of God is His unmerited favor shown to unworthy sinners. No one who has experienced divine grace—and many millions have experienced it—deserved to receive it. The reason they did not deserve it is that all were sinners when it was shown to them. They received it in widely different circumstances. Some, like John Newton, had lived wickedly, showing love to neither God nor human, but they met God through the gospel and discovered that they could be forgiven. Others, such as John Wesley, struggled with self-righteousness until God showed them that salvation was by grace alone, and they too discovered that God could freely pardon them.

The experience of divine grace is not limited to the time when people are converted. Their conversions are only the commencement of the experience of grace that they will know while they are in this world. God will be constantly involved in their lives, forgiving them their sins, guiding them through stages, instructing them from His Word, listening to their prayers, and in many more ways. And His numerous involvements will be expressions of His grace.

Paul reminds Titus that the grace of God has appeared, and he means that it appeared when the Son of God came into the world. This appearance of God's grace was not unexpected as far as the biblical explanation is concerned. In the Bible, we are told clearly that God had planned to reveal His grace in the way that He did, and His plan was prophesied and pictured in the Old Testament. Then it appeared in person in the life and ministry of Jesus, and since His ascension, it has been preached throughout the world by His servants.

Grace Saves

Although "salvation has appeared to all men," Paul does not mean that all people, in the sense of every person, will experience salvation. Rather, he means that the gospel is declared to all, with the aim that each hearer will accept the message and turn to God in repentance, trusting in Jesus for the forgiveness of his or her sins. God does not hinder anyone from coming to Him because they belong to a particular race or social level. Instead, He invites all to receive the blessings of the gospel for themselves.

Salvation is a big topic in the Bible and in the experience of sinners. Many large volumes of theology and many shorter works have been written about it. Countless hymns and songs have warmed the hearts of God's people who have rejoiced to sing about it, whether in large crowds or in small groups. One helpful way of summarizing salvation is the often-used triad that speaks of salvation from the punishment of sin, salvation from the power of sin, and salvation from the presence of sin. We will think about them more closely later, but before we do, we can add another three thoughts to the description: first, salvation planned; second, salvation prophesied; and third, salvation procured.

When was salvation planned by God? The answer to the question is that it was planned in eternity before the universe was created. There are great mysteries connected to this plan, mysteries that we cannot explain. It is sufficient to say that God's plan was an expression of His wisdom, His sovereignty, and His love. He is the all-wise God and capable of knowing intuitively the best plan; He is the sovereign God who could freely choose to enact the best plan; and He is the loving God who could fully express His love in and through His plan. And He did through His grace.

For thousands of years, God indicated through prophecy that salvation was coming. Those predictions are found in the Old Testament. The first prediction was given in the garden of Eden, after the fall of Adam into the state of sin, when God said that One would come and deal with the problems caused by Satan and sin (Gen. 3:15). Numerous other prophecies were given about this promised One who would bring blessing to the world, who would be of the line of Abraham through Isaac, Jacob, Judah, and David. He would be born of a virgin in Bethlehem, would be guided by the Spirit throughout His life on earth, would offer His life as an atonement for sin, would be raised from the dead, and would rule over the world. All those prophecies and countless more were fulfilled in Jesus Christ the Savior.

The focal point of this salvation, the way it was procured, was when the Sufferer endured tremendous punishment at the hand of God. The Gospels detail how this took place at Calvary when Jesus suffered on the cross. There He became a curse, enduring the judgment of God. Psalm 22 tells us what the Sufferer felt inwardly when on the cross, and Isaiah 53 gives an onlooker's view that sees much more than what could be observed visibly by those literally standing beside the cross. Suffice to say that Jesus paid the penalty the Father required of Him. His resurrection, three days later, is the evidence that the Father had accepted His work of salvation; His subsequent ascension and exaltation to the throne of God are the reward He received from the Father, and from there He arranges for salvation to be experienced by sinners as He builds His church.

What happens in the lives of those sinners? This is where the triad mentioned earlier comes in. The first aspect is that all those sinners are delivered from the penalty of sin. They respond to the gospel by faith and rest on Jesus alone for salvation. Immediately, they are pardoned by God the Father in His capacity as judge. He declares them to be justified. This doctrine has a twofold content: in addition to the Father forgiving them, He also reckons to their account the perfect righteousness of Jesus (the perfect life that He lived on earth). The Father's action here is all of grace. Those sinners did not deserve to be forgiven or reckoned righteous in such a way. But all who truly believe in Jesus are.

The second aspect of the triad is that those who believe in Jesus are delivered from the power of sin by the sanctification of the Spirit, who indwells each of them. This deliverance is a lifelong process in which, to quote the Westminster Shorter Catechism, Christians "are renewed in the whole man after the image of God, and are enabled more and more to die unto sin, and live unto righteousness." The work of the Spirit is to conform them to the image of Christ as they become increasingly like Him. Often, they don't think this is the case because one effect of the Spirit's work is to show them how sinful they are. But through the grace of God, they become holier as life continues.

Nevertheless, despite their imperfect sanctification, they will yet experience the third aspect of the triad, which is that they will be saved from the presence of sin. As far as their souls are concerned, this will occur when they die and their souls go to heaven to be with Jesus. Then when Jesus returns, their bodies will be resurrected, reunited with their souls, and they will be glorified in body and soul. Their glorification will be all of grace. Some believers will not have died before Jesus returns, and on that day they will be transformed into His likeness without having to taste death. Their transformation too will be all of grace.

Grace Trains

Paul elaborates on the second aspect of the triad when he writes in Titus 2:12, "teaching us that, denying ungodliness and worldly lusts, we should live soberly, righteously, and godly in the present age." He will continue to refer to salvation from the power of sin in verse 14, and also later in the letter (for example, in 3:4–8). The teaching or training that Paul has in mind is more than passing on information. He includes knowing what is right along with learning how to practice what is right.

The apostle reminds Christians of their responsibility to be fully involved in the ongoing process of their personal sanctification. Their training is a constant activity of the grace of God, a reminder that personal choices have to be made continually. The apostle does not indicate that Christians graduate, as it were, in this life. Rather, the graduation will take place when Jesus returns. Until then, they will be under training according to the grace of God.

It is interesting that Paul includes himself and Titus as among those who attend the classes in God's school ("teaching *us*"; emphasis added). Although he and Titus had special roles as teachers of God's people, he knew that they were responsible to set a good example to other believers. They had to make similar choices regarding holiness of life.

For how long do they need this training? Paul says it is necessary throughout "the present age." There should never be a day when a believer misses out on being taught by grace. Growing older does not reduce the hours of attendance to this training. Indeed, believers find that this divine training is needed and provided wherever they are.

The responsibilities highlighted in the lifelong process fall into negative and positive categories. Negatively, believers have to make a definite choice to renounce ungodliness and worldly passions. The necessity of having to renounce them indicates that there will be a recurring temptation to engage in them. Each time a temptation comes, they must say no to it. Grace never trains a believer to tolerate sin, to experiment with sin, to excuse sin. All sin is a danger, and it must be avoided.

A preacher once told the story of a duchess who was looking for a suitable person to control the horses that pulled her carriage. On the route to her mansion, the road went near the edge of a steep cliff. She asked those who applied for the post how safely they could negotiate that part of the road. One man said that he could drive the carriage safely while only a yard from the edge. Another man said that he could drive the carriage safely while only a foot from the edge. The man who was given the post said that he would keep as far from the edge as possible. When it comes to sin, the safest response is a definite no, a determination not to engage in it in any way.

In contrast, believers are trained by grace to live "soberly, righteously, and godly." It is possible that Paul intended "soberly" to describe what believers do for themselves, "righteously" for how believers treat others, and "godly" for how believers relate to God. Day by day, hour by hour, all Christians should live in a manner that is pleasing to God. That they are sober does not indicate holiness requires loss of emotion. They say no to worldly passions, but they discover that the ways of righteousness bring joy and pleasure to their renewed hearts.

When believers live in this manner, they reveal that their lives have been trained by the grace of God. In some countries, it is the practice for school pupils to wear a uniform that indicates which school they attend. The uniform that Christians should wear is lives that are sober, righteous, and godly. When they have this uniform on, people will know who their Master and teacher is—the God of grace.

10

Hope Possessed Because of Redemption Provided

TITUS 2:13–14a

---

[13]*Looking for the blessed hope and glorious appearing of our great God and Savior Jesus Christ,* [14a]*who gave Himself for us, that He might redeem us from every lawless deed and purify for Himself His own special people, zealous for good works.*

Sometimes we discover a person is much greater than we actually thought when we first saw him. The subsequent discovery of his dignity not only changed our estimation of his person but also enabled us to assess his previous activities in a new light. This can happen in the world of business when a person from a poor background becomes wealthy and uses her wealth for the benefit of others; it can happen in the world of sports when a person with little advantage becomes a champion and reveals the steps he took to become skilled.

There are different ways of considering the greatness of Jesus. We can start with His eternal dignity and work forward and recognize that who He is gives authenticity and quality to His life on earth. Or we can begin with His second coming and look back and realize that His glory, which will be revealed when He returns, is connected to what happened when He was crucified, when He redeemed and purified His people. And becoming aware of what He did then affects us as we respond to Him now.

The Second Coming of Jesus

Paul says two things about the second coming of Jesus. First, he tells us what our attitude should be: we are "looking for the blessed hope." Second, he tells us what we will see: the "glorious appearing of our great God and Savior Jesus Christ."

Hope is essential for healthy living. When a person loses hope, perhaps through ill health or bereavement or financial bankruptcy, it is very difficult for her to see anything positive in life. Everything becomes dark, and the future is bleak. But if a person has something to look forward to, such as a wedding or the birth of a child or coming into an inheritance, then there is buoyancy and optimism in her life.

Christians have a hope. Sometimes it is described as "a living hope" (1 Peter 1:3); here, it is "a blessed hope." It will be an occasion that will be marked by joyful blessings. Believers will be resurrected from the dead, will be reunited with one another, will be sinless and holy, and will be glorified. It will be the commencement of the life of the ages, eternal life in its fullness. The new heavens and new earth will appear.

Such certainly is a great hope to possess, one that enables believers to cope with the difficulties and disappointments of life. They know that, as others have said, "the best is yet to be." Their experience will not always be what it currently is because even the best of times now can be marred. A great future is ahead of them, a future that is impossible to describe in all its beauty and fullness. But the hope connected to that future burns within their hearts.

Paul reminds Titus that they are "*looking* for the blessed hope" (emphasis added). The attitude of "looking" reveals certain features. Obviously, there is a conviction that the desired event will definitely occur. In addition, "looking" indicates the necessity of patience until it happens. And the willingness to look points to an anticipation that the occurrence will be worthwhile when it comes to pass. If that were not the case, why would someone look for it? In Romans 8, while writing about the future renewal of creation, Paul stresses how to focus on it: "But if we hope for what we do not see, we eagerly wait for it with perseverance" (v. 25). The fulfillment of the hope will reveal that it was worth waiting for.

Paul focuses on one amazing feature of that great future day when Jesus returns and His people gather in His presence. The feature that he highlights concerns the "glorious appearing of our great God and Savior Jesus Christ." This statement is very full.[1] Its range of titles describe the deity and the humanity of the Savior. Paul says that it will be a day when Jesus will be seen in an awesome manner.

What will be seen on that day is the glory of Jesus. A foretaste of this experience was given to Peter, James, and John on the Mount of Transfiguration when they saw the glory of Jesus for a short time (Matt. 17:1–8). Jesus had prayed about His glory on the evening of His arrest: "And now, O Father, glorify Me together with Yourself, with the glory which I had with You before the world was" (John 17:5). That prayer was answered at His ascension to the Father's right hand, and since then His glory has been visible to the inhabitants of heaven. On the day that He returns, His glory will be seen by all His creatures, and they will recognize that He is indeed the divine Savior, God and man.

We live between the two appearings of Jesus, and Paul mentions both in this paragraph. In verse 11, he refers to the first coming of Jesus, when the grace of God was revealed in the life of service given by the Savior. We look back with wonder at what He did for us in His life and death. But we also look ahead to His return and anticipate with joy the recognition that will be given to Him then.

How will we react when He is revealed in glory before our eyes? Surely our response will be enthralled worship. Isaiah was overwhelmed when he was given a brief experience of being in the presence of the glory of Jesus (Isaiah 6; John 12:41). The prophet realized how sinful he was on that occasion. When the future event

---

1. There has been disagreement about the meaning of the phrase "our great God and Savior Jesus Christ." Some say that two persons are indicated here—one is God the Father, and the other is Jesus Christ the Savior. Others point out that the pronoun "our" describes both God and Savior, so stating very clearly the full deity of Jesus Christ.

comes, it will not be brief but endless. Instead of a deep sense of sinfulness, Jesus's people will be transformed into His likeness and glorified along with Him forevermore, although they will not become divine. The thought of being with Jesus, our great God and Savior, should be overwhelming as we anticipate the outcome of His grace.

The Purchase of His People

Paul returns to write about the first coming of Jesus and why He went to the cross. He died on the cross to redeem His people. "Redemption" refers to the purchase of someone or something, usually by paying a financial price. In the case of Jesus, however, the price was not financial but personal. He "gave Himself for us."

How do we describe His self-giving? He gave Himself freely because He was not compelled to do so by any external power. Out of His love for His Father and for His people, He agreed to give Himself, and that is why He became a man. He knew what He was doing, and He did so willingly, even though the experience on the cross would be very distressing.

Moreover, Jesus gave Himself fully as well as freely. He offered Himself without spot to God. He held nothing back. His whole heart and strength went into His action of paying the price. He went as far as He had to go in order to pay it. It is impossible for us to put a value on it except to say that it was infinite. He satisfied the demands of divine justice. Only He was capable of paying it, and He did.

This means that Jesus, as well as giving Himself freely and fully, also gave Himself finally. He had to do it only once. Since the price has been paid for the redemption of His people, the God of justice will never require it again. We can look at Jesus today and contemplate the one who, out of His great love for us, redeemed us freely, fully, and finally.

What were we redeemed from? Paul describes our state as lawless. In other words, we were rebels against our God. We had disobeyed His laws deliberately, and that disobedience was inward as well as outward. Moreover, it was increasing all the time. Our disobedience had put us in a prison with no prospect of ever being able to find a way of release. The prison was the state of sin, and all we did in that state was to keep on sinning, increasing our guilt and the penalty we had to pay. We truly were slaves of sin, requiring a remarkable Redeemer. And although we did not realize that our Redeemer existed, He knew that we would exist, and He came to pay the price that sets us free from the grip of lawlessness.

Paul assures us that the redeeming work of Jesus dealt with whatever sins we were guilty of. None of us are exactly the same as another person, and even though we have all broken the same law, we have not all broken it in the same manner. Yet Paul states clearly that Jesus redeemed His people from "every lawless deed." As far as the offended Judge is concerned, the price has been paid and they are set free.

What was the intended outcome of this redemption? What did the Redeemer have in mind for those He liberated? Although He delivered them from lawlessness, they were not set free from all authority. Rather, they became His property, His possession. He purchased them in order for them to be a pure people, suitable to serve Him, cleansed by His blood.

God's Special People

Paul uses a description, "his own special people" (v. 14), that was used of Israel in the Old Testament. God regarded them as His special people: "For you are a holy people to the LORD your God, and the LORD has chosen you to be a people for Himself, a special treasure above all the peoples who are on the face of the earth" (Deut. 14:2). It is clear from this description that believers are very dear to God.

Paul has already reminded Titus of several ways in which the Lord revealed His love for His people. In eternity past, He had chosen them to be His, a reminder that His love for them had no beginning. Although they were sinners, Jesus came into the world and paid a great price to redeem them so that they would be His purified people. And they can look forward to the second coming of Jesus, when they will enter into the inheritance that He will give to them as His people.

Sometimes Christians are so overwhelmed by their sinfulness that they forget who they are. Can it be the case that Jesus still wants them as His people? He did not discover their sinfulness only when they discovered it. He has known all along who they are and what they are like. Their sinfulness does not reduce His love for them. It is His intention to present them spotless at the end of the day. Then they will be like Him. As the German hymn writer Gerhardt Tersteegen wrote,

> He, who in the hour of sorrow,
> Bore the curse alone;
> I who through the lonely desert,
> Trod where He had gone.
> He and I in that bright glory,
> One deep joy shall share.
> Mine, to be forever with Him.
> His, that I am there.[2]

Responding to Jesus

Let us reflect on Paul's description of believers. They have a great future described as "the blessed hope"; they have been redeemed from the state of sin and cleansed from the defilement that their sins caused; they have been purchased to be Jesus's possession forever. Surely the only response is to dedicate themselves to the Savior in a spirit marked by deep gratitude and intense love.

One of the great privileges of the Christian life is that we don't only live *for* Jesus, but that we can also live *with* Jesus. People who live together speak with one another and share their opinions and values. It is good for us to say, "I must live for Jesus." It is also good for us to speak to Him as one whom we know closely and love dearly, the one who gave Himself in the past at the cross so that He

2. Gerhardt Tersteegen, "Till He Come," in the public domain.

could continually give His great blessing to His own special possession, His beloved people.

Who can say or estimate how much Jesus wants to be with us? A glance at His invitation to the believers in Laodicea, as He knocks loudly at the door of their lives, tells us: "Behold, I stand at the door and knock. If anyone hears My voice and opens the door, I will come in to him and dine with him, and he with Me" (Rev. 3:20). Maybe He is knocking today.

11

Zealous for Good Works

TITUS 2:14b

[14b] *Zealous for good works.*

Why did Jesus redeem and cleanse His people? Several answers could be given to that question, such as He loved them eternally, He was sent by the Father to redeem them, and He wanted them to be with Him forever. Another answer is that He wanted them to live devoted lives for the glory of God, and Paul has this answer in mind when he says to Titus that the Christians in Crete, who had been converted recently, should be zealous for good works.

Regarding zeal, there are certain qualifications that should be made. It is obvious that merely being zealous by itself could be dangerous. There must be both right motives and right goals in doing whatever we are zealous about. Therefore, we must concentrate on what is right, and Paul says that what we should be zealous about is good works. He does not mean only acts of charity, which is how the term "good works" is often used today. Good works, as we have seen already in this letter, are the opposite of sinful activities.

Definitions of Christian Zeal

It will be useful to read some definitions of Christian zeal. J. C. Ryle wrote an essay on such zeal. Christian zeal, he said, "is a burning desire to please God, to do His will, and to advance His glory in the world in every possible way. It is a desire, which is not natural to men or women. It is a desire which the Spirit puts in the heart of every believer when they are converted to Christ, however, a desire which some believers feel so much more strongly than others that they alone deserve to be called 'zealous' men and women."

Ryle continued:

> A zealous person in Christianity is pre-eminently a person of one thing. It is not enough to say that they are earnest, strong, uncompromising, meticulous, wholehearted, and fervent in spirit. They only see one thing, they care for one thing, they live for one thing, they are swallowed up in one thing; and that one thing is to please God. Whether they live, or whether they die—whether they are healthy, or whether they are sick—whether they are rich, or whether they are poor—whether they please man, or whether they give offense—whether they are thought wise, or whether they are thought foolish—whether they are accused, or whether they are praised—whether they get honor, or whether they get shame—for all this the zealous person cares nothing at all. They have a passion for one thing, and that one thing is to please God and to advance God's glory.[1]

When I became a Christian several decades ago, one of the popular authors at that time was William MacDonald, who authored the book *True Discipleship*. He began a chapter on zeal with these words: "A disciple can be forgiven if he does not have great mental ability. He can be forgiven also if he does not display outstanding physical prowess. But no disciple can be excused if he does not have zeal. If his heart is not aflame with a red-hot passion for the Saviour, he stands condemned."[2]

Biblical Description of a Zealous Person

Who do we look for when we want a role model who exemplifies

---

1. J. C. Ryle, "Zeal," in *Practical Religion* (London: William Hunt, 1887), 184–85.

2. William MacDonald, "Zeal," in *True Discipleship* (1962; repr., [Port Colborne, Ont.]: Gospel Folio Press, 2003), chap. 5, digital book.

living for God? The first person to consider would be Jesus because He is our best example. Then we should consider examples of Bible characters who are commended for their zeal as well as Bible verses that require zeal in believers.

An incident in which Jesus revealed His zeal is recorded in John 2:13–22, where He showed great zeal in removing sinful practices from the temple. He overthrew the tables where people exchanged money, and He drove out the animals. Initially, people may have been surprised by what Jesus did because money was needed to pay temple taxes and the animals were needed for offering sacrifices. Yet He saw that the sellers were not interested in the things of God but in making a commercial gain. In contrast, He was consumed with His Father's glory, and He knew that those wrong practices should be removed from the temple. So His fervency and zeal for God led Him to act. No doubt many truths can be seen in His response, but we can mention that His zeal displayed righteous indignation that the things of God were being used for ill-gotten gain. He did not merely criticize; He also confronted the issue. And He did so with fervor, without losing control.

A Bible character who is commended for his zeal is Phinehas, the grandson of Aaron, who was commended by God for executing a man who was defiling the people of Israel through a blatant expression of immorality (Num. 25:1–18). His action in doing so was pleasing to God and removed the need for further divine judgment. He showed true zeal because he was committed to the honor of God. This is a basic requirement that also expresses love for God.

Jesus called the worldly church in Laodicea to repent of their sins toward Him. What kind of repentance did He require? He said they should have zealous repentance (Rev. 3:19). This must mean that there should be energy in it, that it should be marked by expressions of eagerness to be restored to a warm relationship with the Savior. While it would not be right to say merely that they had to work at repentance, it is right to say that their repentance required passion as they lamented their failures and sought forgiveness for them. Such fervent repentance comes from God through the working of the Spirit. Yet since Jesus called them to possess and express such repentance, we can expect Him to answer pleas for it.

A fourth reference to zeal is mentioned by Paul in Romans 12:11 (ESV): "Do not be slothful in zeal, be fervent in spirit, serve the Lord." There is a strong similarity between zeal and fervency of spirit, and we can only serve the Lord suitably when we have such eagerness in our hearts. In verse 8, Paul had called on leaders to lead with zeal (sometimes translated "diligence"), and in verse 11 he says that zeal should be a mark of all believers.

From these four biblical references, we can see that people with true zeal put God first, are distressed when His ways and requirements are ignored, do something about the wrong practice, feel strongly when they personally repent, and serve the Lord with enthusiasm. In showing true zeal, such people are Christlike, pleasing to God, and meaningful contributors to church life.

Paul, as we know, was by nature a zealous man. He revealed that this was part of his temperament in the way that he persisted in persecuting the church. Did this mean that when he was converted, his natural zeal, now renewed, began to reveal itself in holy ways? I would say yes. Then what about unconverted people who seem passive and disengaged about most things? What happens to them after conversion? I would say that an essential feature of authentic humanity, which had been asleep when they were unconverted, becomes alive through the work of the Spirit and shows itself in dedicated and loving service of the Lord.

Zealous for Good Works

We know that words change their meaning over time through adjustments in everyday use. One such change has occurred with the idea of good works. Today, the description is almost a synonym for works of charity, of occasional expressions of neighborly kindness. Since the meaning has changed, it is possible for us to insert the contemporary meaning into the biblical statement and misunderstand what the verse means.

Paul refers to good works several times in this brief letter. He says in Titus 1:16 that false teachers are "disqualified for every good work." Titus himself is told to be "a pattern of good works" (2:7). In Titus 3:1, the good works of Christians should commend them to the government, and in verse 8 they are to "be careful to maintain good works." The requirement in verse 8 is virtually the same as the statement "be zealous for good works." We can see from those references that Paul regarded good works as essential for Christians.

So what are the good works that Paul expects the Cretan believers to perform? The basic answer is that they are what God requires from us in the commandments of His Word. When practiced for the right reasons, they are expressions of love for God and for people.

It is important that they are practiced for right motives. A person can give a gift to someone hoping for something in return. That is not a right motive, and it disqualifies the action from being a good work, even if it seems a correct one. Or he could do something because he wanted other people to think he is better than others. That, again, is not a right motive.

What is the most powerful motive for doing good works, for obeying the commandments of God? The motive must come from gratitude to the God who planned our salvation, who sent His Son to be the Savior, who brought us from death to life by the Holy Spirit, and who promises to bring us eventually to glory.

It is easy to see what a good work is from a biblical point of view. But why should we be zealous about doing them? Here are four reasons.

First, living in this way is a very good witness to the grace of God. Others will see how great the change in our lives has been. People often will not hear our words, but if they know us, they will see our lives. They will wonder why we live as we do. Such living is attractive. A happy Christian living a devoted life engaged in good activities is a powerful witness to the gospel. Jesus said to His disciples in Matthew 5:16, "Let your light so shine before men, that they may see your good works and glorify your Father in heaven."

Second, the desire to perform such activities and the performance of them is a powerful contribution to one's assurance. While Christians know that such actions are not perfect, they also know that they would not have done them before their conversion. They are evidences of the great change that has taken place. And when they find in their heart such eagerness to do these good works, they see that the Spirit has been working within them to give them such desires.

Third, when Christians are zealous for good works, they help other Christians to become zealous as well. Those looking on, who perhaps are a bit fearful of doing some good works, realize that they can be done in a manner that glorifies God.

Fourth, the practice of good works is an expression of Christlikeness. Jesus said about Himself in John 10:32, "Many good works I have shown you from My Father. For which of those works do you stone Me?" Peter described the ministry of Jesus when he said that "God anointed Jesus of Nazareth with the Holy Spirit and with power, who went about doing good and healing all who were oppressed by the devil, for God was with Him" (Acts 10:38).

Our Response

We have all failed at some time or even many times to do good works that please God. Since that is the case, we should come to God, confess our failures, and ask for His forgiveness. We may have had to many times, but we can still come again to God in repentance and then be zealous for good works.

12

Living in Society

TITUS 2:15–3:3

2:15 Speak these things, exhort, and rebuke with all authority. Let no one despise you.

3:1 Remind them to be subject to rulers and authorities, to obey, to be ready for every good work, 3:2 to speak evil of no one, to be peaceable, gentle, showing all humility to all men. 3:3 For we ourselves were also once foolish, disobedient, deceived, serving various lusts and pleasures, living in malice and envy, hateful and hating one another.

Sometimes we wonder why chapter divisions in the Bible are where they are. Obviously, they make it easy for readers to locate a passage. Yet the divisions may also separate verses that should be together. In the last verse of Titus 2, Paul used four verbs to describe how Titus should communicate the message that he had been given by God ("speak," "exhort," "rebuke," and "let no one despise"). In the first verse of chapter 3, Paul uses a fifth verb, "remind." It looks as if the five verbs should be together, describing how Titus should preach.

How to Preach

The obvious feature of this list of verbs is that a preacher has to be aware of the full authority he possesses as the messenger of Christ to ensure conformity to his Master's will in His church. His authority is not found in himself but because he has been commissioned by God. The material that he has authority to declare is what is found under the sound doctrine that Paul has been explaining earlier in the letter; in other words, what God says in His Word.

Moreover, the list demands Titus insist that his message must be heard by those to whom it applies, and he should not allow anyone to try to avoid understanding the truth and becoming aware of their responsibility to apply personally what is demanded of him or her. And we can see that the list also requires clarity in what the preacher says because there is a clear difference between exhorting and rebuking.

Before a preacher delivers his message, he must know some things about his listeners; otherwise, his exhortations may not be suitable, and his rebukes may be irrelevant. When he is applying biblical passages, he must stress what is stated in them, but the verbs that Paul is using indicate that Titus has to address particular situations accurately.

Care is required when preparing a message to ensure that its contents are applied as they should be. It is possible to declare the truth without exhorting or rebuking. It is also possible to exhort or rebuke without paying attention to what a passage says. A writer in the *Biblical Illustrator* used the case of a general preparing for battle to illustrate the care that a pastor should give in composing his sermons. The general surveyed the terrain, observed where dangers might be, and arranged his weapons. The preacher should think about his listeners beforehand and where they are in a spiritual sense. There will always be some who need encouragement and some who need correction.

There is always the possibility that a preacher God sends can be despised by his listeners. Paul himself was aware of what that was like. He had encountered people, especially in Corinth, who had attempted to demean him and dismiss him because he did not use the methods common to traveling orators (2 Cor. 11:6). Others despised his physical appearance (2 Cor. 10:10). But he did not let their attitude minimize his God-given authority.

As was the case with Titus, it is part of a pastor's task to remind the church frequently of such matters, not only because the church members might be in danger of forgetting but also because of the importance of the subjects themselves. Important matters should be repeated again and again so that Christians have them clearly in their minds and know how they should behave as well as what they should believe.

Living Differently

It is the case that most people expect Christians to live differently from other people. Usually, they will not see the way that believers behave in church and observe the way they interact with one another. But their lives should be a witness in their communities that they have been born again. Paul was probably aware of many situations in which this would happen, but since he was composing a brief letter, he chose to highlight crucial principles that would cover most areas of contact with those who are not believers.

The list of topics in Titus 3:1–2 is concerned with practical Christian living. Although Paul's list of subjects is short, it is also comprehensive, ranging from how a Christian should respond to civic authorities to how he or she should interact with other people. In his instructions in chapters 1 and 2, Paul had mainly focused on how believers should behave within the church and the family, but now he highlights their behavior among those who are outside the church. He is dealing with an essential aspect of ongoing sanctification, detailing evidences that indicate a person is a genuine Christian.

This is a reminder that Christians are citizens of two kingdoms. They belong to the kingdom of God, and they also live in a political system of one kind or another. The society in which the Cretans lived was not ideal as far as Christians were concerned. Yet they had to live for Christ within that location. How would they do so?

Be Submissive

The first area of public life that Paul mentions is *submission to rulers and authorities*. This is a surprising requirement in a sense because Paul frequently had suffered unjustly at the hands of rulers and had only recently been released from imprisonment in Rome. It is well known that the Roman authorities could be barbaric—we only have to think of crucifixion to recognize this or to think about the cruelty that was shown to slaves.

So why does Paul insist on civic obedience? He knows that human authority is a divine institution. Paul was not living in what we call a Christian society, nor was he living in a society that valued human rights, yet as he makes clear in Romans 13:1–7, he recognized that he was living in a society in which God had placed certain individuals in positions of authority. To disobey them if their requirements were not contrary to God's laws was to disobey God, and such a response is not merely rebellion against rulers but also an expression of rebellion against God.

Jesus taught that it was right to recognize civic authorities. In Matthew 22:15–22, there is an account of an incident in which some opponents of Jesus tried to trap Him by asking if it was lawful according to Jewish law to pay a poll tax to Caesar. They imagined that if He said it was, He would be guilty of disregarding the Jewish law; and if He said it was not, He would be disobeying the Roman law. Jesus easily dealt with their trivial question by saying that we should render to Caesar the things that are his and to God the things that are His. Jesus's answer makes it clear that it is right to recognize human authorities as fulfilling a God-given role.

Paul was not suggesting that civic authorities should be obeyed when they advocate laws that are wrong. When that happens, as Peter and John said in Acts 5:29, Christians have to obey God rather than men. Nevertheless, Paul is saying that Christians normally should be noted for their willingness to acknowledge those whom God in providence has placed in situations of power. Indeed, such should be their interest in those in power that they should regularly pray for them, especially with regard to how rulers should tolerate the gospel and godly living (1 Tim. 2:1–3).

In previous generations, Western society was willing to submit to the authority of rulers. Today it is different, and there is a strong antagonism to authority, with many people doing what they themselves think right. Christians are not to be like that. Instead, they recognize that God has given authority to rulers. At the time Paul wrote this letter, it is likely that Nero was the Roman emperor. He was a sinful, cruel ruler who later on maltreated believers in an appalling manner. Yet his behavior was not a reason for Christians rejecting the belief that human authorities are ordained by God.

The next requirement that Paul says should be taught is *the necessity of obedience.* It may be the case that he is repeating the submission to civic authorities, perhaps with an emphasis on inner heart obedience in addition to outward conformity. Two comments may explain why he mentions this form of obedience. First, people's mere outward submission will not last long, and they will easily move away from it. Second, there was a strong spirit of rebellion in Crete against the Roman authority,[1] and it could influence Christians living there. Believers are always prone to engage in what they see around them in the lives of others, and there would have been a temptation in Crete to participate in anti-government activities. Therefore, Paul uses a double exhortation—to submit and to obey—to indicate the importance and necessity of doing what the civic authorities decree.

Be Ready

William Hendriksen comments that "the expression 'ready for every good work' forms a natural bridge between the duties which believers owe to their government and those which they owe to their neighbors."[2] If that is the case, it means that Christians should be ready to participate in public activities organized by those in power as long as they can be classified as good. This is one way they can

---

1. John Stott cites a comment by William Barclay, who wrote, "Paul is possibly glancing at the notoriously turbulent character of the Cretans, of which Polybius tells us; they were constantly involved in 'insurrections, murders and internecine wars.'" John R. W. Stott, *The Message of 1 Timothy and Titus: God's Good News for the World*, Bible Speaks Today (Leicester, England: Inter-Varsity Press, 1996), comment on Titus 3:1.

2. William Hendriksen, *New Testament Commentary: Exposition of I and II Thessalonians [and] Exposition of the Pastoral Epistles*, New Testament Commentary (Grand Rapids: Baker, 1979), comment on Titus 3:1.

function as salt and light in society, by taking part in suitable careers and endeavors that enhance daily living. Christians with such suitable gifts should be ready when called on to do so.

Readiness must include suitable preparation. Perhaps a Christian has an interest in politics and is becoming aware that God is calling him to fulfill that role in society. If he cannot see how the door will open, he should still prepare so as to be ready when it does open. The principle of being ready can be extended to many areas of life. There is something wrong with a Christian who is not ready to do what is good and especially in areas of life for which he or she is gifted to contribute.

Readiness also includes the willingness to get involved in improving circumstances in society. There are numerous examples of modern charities that were founded by Christians who saw a need that had to be addressed. For example, in the nineteenth century, Christians in the United Kingdom were involved in the commencement of societies to look after children in need, to care for people with physical difficulties, and to ensure the welfare of animals.[3]

Getting involved in what is good is not limited to such activities. There will be ample opportunities for Christians and churches to engage in good activities that strengthen the effects of their witness to the Lord as well as participating in ways that reveal God's provisions given through His common grace.

Be Gentle

In addition to seeing a Christian engaged in doing good, those outside the church should see four features, two that are negative and two that are positive. The negatives are "to speak evil of no one" and "to be peaceable." We can easily understand the relevance of such reminders to people who used to be liars and like wild beasts (Titus 1:12). Here we have another example from the Bible regarding how Christians are not to use their tongues.

---

3. Geoffrey Hanks describes the origins of several such societies in his book *60 Great Founders* (Fearn, Ross-shire, Scotland: Christian Focus, 1995).

Paul is not suggesting that they should not evaluate or assess other people, but he is asserting that they cannot say what is untrue and slanderous.[4] Moreover, by using a word that means "to slander," Paul indicates that believers should have a high estimation of other humans, avoiding disrespectful or demeaning comments about them. Paul may still have civic rulers in mind, but the verse as a whole would indicate that he is now referring to people in general.

In Paul's time there may have been a tendency among Christians to look down on others because they were still idolaters worshiping nonexistent gods and to cast aspersions on such people. There are an endless number of such scenarios. In whatever way such slanderous speaking is done, it is wrong. And believers who practice this reduce the effectiveness of their Christian witness.

The second negative ("to avoid quarreling" [ESV]) and the first positive ("to be…gentle") are linked together. A quarrelsome person is not a gentle person. These two qualities are mentioned in 1 Timothy 3:3 as necessary for an elder, but here they describe what every Christian's inner attitude should be, which is a reminder that the same standards are required of laypeople as elders. People quarrel verbally because they have a quarrelsome spirit, whereas people respond gently because they have a gentle spirit. (Other Bible translations use the term "peaceable" instead of "not quarreling.")

The term translated as "gentle" has a variety of emphases, such as kind and deferential; one common suggestion is sweet reasonableness. It is straightforward to see here a call for Christlikeness because Christ was gentle and lowly in heart (Matt. 11:29), and He did not quarrel, even with those who reviled Him when He was arrested and mistreated.

---

4. The word translated as "speak evil" is *blasphemein*. Fairburn comments that the word "imports more than to speak evil in the ordinary sense; it is to act the part of a reviler or slanderer; and when used of conduct from one man toward another, always betokens the exercise of a very bitter and malignant spirit." Patrick Fairburn, *The Pastoral Epistles: The Greek Text and Translation* (Edinburgh: T&T Clark, 1874), 289.

The second positive, "showing all humility to all men," is an outworking of a gentle spirit.[5] It is to be visible ("showing"), continual (present tense), and general ("to all men"). No matter who we meet, no matter their disposition, Christians are always to remain respectful and gentle.

As I noted when considering verse 1, some may be surprised that Paul exhorts his readers to submit to a pagan government. Some may also be surprised at his insistence that God's people should have gentle characters and show respect to everyone. Yet when we think about it, we can see that Paul is urging Titus to remind his listeners that Jesus calls them to live a totally different kind of life, one that is unique as far as this world is concerned.

Be Grateful

Paul does not forget what believers, including Titus and himself, were like before they experienced God's grace: "For we ourselves were also once foolish, disobedient, deceived, serving various lusts and pleasures, living in malice and envy, hateful and hating one another" (Titus 3:3). They were guilty of the same sins that unconverted people in Crete were currently practicing. Recollection of who they were should cause Christians to be humble and compassionate toward those who have not experienced God's mercy. Observing the sins of others should be accompanied by an awareness that at one time they, too, were lost in sin. Inevitably they should be grateful to the God who has saved them.

Paul does not mean that unbelievers lack intellectual ability when he describes them as foolish. Rather, he means that they did not possess the true wisdom that would lead them to obey God or other authorities. Since that was the case, it was inevitable that they would be led astray and indulge in various expressions of sinful behavior, including constant dislike and jealousy of others.

---

5. The word translated as "humility" is *prauteta*, and it is sometimes translated as "gentleness." Paul strengthens *prauteta* with the word *pasan*, which means "every kind of" and is here translated as "all."

Spurgeon, in a sermon on this passage, commented about the society of his time in this manner:

> When we look upon the world today, it pains us by its folly, disobedience and delusion. He that knows most of this modern Babylon, whether he observes the richer or the poorer classes of society, will find the deepest cause for grief. But we cannot condemn with bitterness—for such were some of us. Not only can we not condemn with bitterness but we must look upon our sinful fellow creatures with great compassion—for such were some of us.[6]

The list that Paul provides reveals the inbuilt depth that sin has ingrained into the hearts of sinners. Reading the list is a reminder of why divine power was needed to deliver believers from their unregenerate state. It is also a reminder as to why there is so much rebellion, conflict, and immorality in the world. Everyone outside of Christ is liable to engage in those sins at any time.

At the same time, the recollection of what they were should encourage believers to share the gospel with unconverted people. They know that it was through the gospel that they experienced the power of God in their lives. Through faith in Jesus, they had been saved from the penalty of their sins and also received the Holy Spirit to indwell them, and His power was revealed in their ongoing salvation.

This is what Paul said to the Corinthian believers after describing the immoral society in which they lived: "And such were some of you. But you were washed, but you were sanctified, but you were justified in the name of the Lord Jesus and by the Spirit of our God" (1 Cor. 6:11). And recollection of his own past can partly explain his words in 1 Timothy 1:15–16: "This is a faithful saying and worthy of all acceptance, that Christ Jesus came into the world

---

6. C. H. Spurgeon, "The Maintenance of Good Works" (sermon on Titus 3:3–8), in *Metropolitan Tabernacle Pulpit*, vol. 34, The Spurgeon Center, "Sermons," https://www.spurgeon.org/resource-library/sermons/the-maintenance-of-good-works/#flipbook/.

to save sinners, of whom I am chief. However, for this reason I obtained mercy, that in me first Jesus Christ might show all longsuffering, as a pattern to those who are going to believe on Him for everlasting life."

Paul says to Titus that he should remind Christians of what they should do and what they should remember. And his instruction comes to us twenty centuries later with the same divine authority.

13

The Grace of the Father

TITUS 3:4–7

---

[4]*But when the kindness and the love of God our Savior toward man appeared,* [5]*not by works of righteousness which we have done, but according to His mercy He saved us, through the washing of regeneration and renewing of the Holy Spirit,* [6]*whom He poured out on us abundantly through Jesus Christ our Savior,* [7]*that having been justified by His grace we should become heirs according to the hope of eternal life.*

Paul has already appealed in this letter to the saving work of God as an incentive for Christian living (Titus 2:11–14). Having again described the desperate state in which believers had been before they were saved (3:3), it is not surprising that Paul then writes a description of the salvation God provided for such sinners.[1] Although he refers to each of the divine persons, he does so from the perspective of what the Father has done for His people.

The Roots of Grace

Paul reminds Titus that the source of salvation is found in the character of God and mentions three of His divine attributes—kindness, love, and mercy. In acting according to those attributes, the Father

1. Some suggest that in 3:4–7, Paul is citing an early doctrinal statement or brief creed. It is also possible that the reference to "faithful saying" in verse 8 refers back to the words in verses 4–7 rather than to what follows.

reveals Himself as Savior, and Paul gives Him that title in verse 4. How can we understand those attributes?

Sometimes, two divine attributes can be similar in meaning and in how they are revealed when God acts in special ways. It is possible that Paul in verse 4 is asking Titus to consider the kindness of God as it is revealed in His compassionate love to the unworthy, whom he has described in the previous verse.

God's kindness to needy sinners can be considered in more than one way. For example, He reveals His kindness to the human race by providing them with what they need for daily life. Paul referred to this expression of divine goodness when addressing the citizens of Lystra (Acts 14:8–18). Those divinely given temporal blessings come under the category of common grace, common because they are given generally to all.

God's kindness is also seen in His plan of salvation whereby sinners experience saving grace, which is the category that Paul describes to Titus in this set of verses. His saving grace reveals His love and kindness in a marvelous way, and Paul stresses this when he describes the Father as "God our Savior." Clearly, Paul wanted Titus to rejoice in God's salvation as he instructed people in Crete about it. As far as Paul was concerned, such knowledge is a powerful incentive to holiness in professing believers.

How Does the Father Save His People?

Paul makes very clear that it is impossible for sinners to save themselves by their own attempts at producing righteousness. No matter how good such an attempt might seem, all their efforts are tainted by sin and are therefore unacceptable to God. Sinners may assume that doing their best will be sufficient, but that will never be the case. Instead, they need salvation from outside themselves, a fact that Paul highlights when he wrote that God's kindness and love had "appeared." It appeared when the Father sent His Son into the world to save sinners.

So how does God save people? The apostle states that the actions of God in salvation are the outworking of His mercy. In the Bible, we read about sovereign mercy when God says that He will have mercy on whom He will have mercy (Rom. 9:15). That statement might seem rather limiting, but we should also bear in mind that the Bible also says that God is rich in mercy (Eph. 2:4). C. H. Spurgeon described divine mercy in this way: "It is great mercy. There is nothing little in my God; His mercy is like Himself—it is infinite. You cannot measure it.... His mercy is so great—that it forgives great sins of great sinners, after great lengths of time—and then gives great favours and great privileges and raises us up to great enjoyments in the great Heaven of the great God!"[2]

In this reference to mercy in this statement about God's great salvation, Paul mentions three blessings that it brings. First is "the washing of regeneration and renewing of the Holy Spirit" (v. 5); second is being "justified by His grace" (v. 7); and third is "heirs according to the hope of eternal life" (v. 7). While those three blessings are distinct, they occur at the moment a person becomes a Christian. Paul refers to the doctrines of regeneration, justification, and adoption.

Regeneration and Renewal

Paul includes the contribution of each of the divine persons here. He tells us that this activity of the Holy Spirit was "poured out on us abundantly through Jesus Christ our Savior." How can we understand this threefold involvement? It can be stated simply: The Father sends the Spirit to people through the agency of Jesus, who is the exalted Mediator in heaven. As the Mediator, He functions as the Prophet, Priest, and King of His people. He did so when He was here on earth, and He continues to do so from His exalted position in heaven.

Jesus promised His disciples that when He ascended to heaven, He would ask the Father for the Holy Spirit, and this request

2. C. H. Spurgeon, "Ben-Hadad's Escape—An Encouragement for Sinners," in *Metropolitan Tabernacle Pulpit*, vol. 9, The Spurgeon Center, "Sermons," https://www.spurgeon.org/resource-library/sermons/ben-hadads-escape-an-encouragement-for-sinners/#flipbook/.

was fulfilled initially when the Holy Spirit was poured forth on the day of Pentecost. On that august occasion, the Holy Spirit strengthened the existing disciples and brought forth new disciples by regenerating over three thousand sinners. The richness of that outpouring is seen in the effects it had on them and on everyone else who has experienced this blessing through the work of the Spirit. How?

Such are washed by the divine work of regeneration. "Regeneration" means "to be reborn, to be given life." Before believers experience this activity of the Spirit, they are dead in trespasses and sins. Their sins make them filthy in the sight of God. Recall the way Paul describes unbelievers in verse 3: "For we ourselves were also once foolish, disobedient, deceived, serving various lusts and pleasures, living in malice and envy, hateful and hating one another."

Those words describe the state of spiritual death. In order to change their state, the Holy Spirit gives them new life, which is the opposite of spiritual death. So regeneration can be likened to a washing because it changes those who experience it. They no longer are the unclean sinners that they were.

Paul also says that the work of the Holy Spirit is a renewal. Regenerated persons are the same individuals as they were before, but they are not the same kind of individuals. They have been remade in each aspect of who they are, although it is important to observe that they are not made perfect at regeneration; they remain sinners, although saved sinners. Still, the renewal by the Holy Spirit is extensive, affecting individuals in their mind, their affections, and their will. They are now a new creation. A radical change has occurred in them, and they have been changed permanently.

We can see that this action of the Holy Spirit is the first step in the process of sanctification. Ahead of a person is a life of progressive sanctification that will occur until his or her life is over, when sanctification is perfected. But the process begins with the gracious activity of the Holy Spirit, sent by Jesus, the Lord of the church, in order that such sinners will experience the riches of the goodness and loving-kindness of the Father.

Justified by His Grace

The second blessing that Paul mentions is the doctrine of justification. This doctrine, or at least the rediscovery of it, was at the heart of the Protestant Reformation. As far as the experience of believers is concerned, justification follows from the work of the Spirit in regeneration, although there is not a time gap between them. When people are regenerated, they trust in Jesus, and when they trust in Jesus, they are justified by the Father.

When we think of justification as an expression of the Father's mercy, we should remind ourselves that justification is the opposite of condemnation. Up until that moment of justification, we were under divine condemnation for our sins; Paul says that we were "children of wrath," even as others (Eph. 2:3). But in an extraordinary display of mercy, God pardons immediately all those who believe in Jesus. It is an instantaneous declaration made in heaven about them rather than an activity that takes place within them after regeneration.

This justification is always a divine pronouncement on an individual. Even if two persons are converted at the same moment in the same room, they are justified by God separately from one another. Each of them possesses the same standing before God, but they have it as individuals. Justification describes the personal standing a believer in Jesus has from the Father and before the Father. And this standing is permanent; it cannot be changed even when the justified sinner disobeys God's law. Why?

The answer to this question is the basis for our justification. When God justifies a sinner, two things happen. One is that all his sins are pardoned for the sake of Christ, and the other is that the righteousness of Jesus is reckoned to the sinner's account. This divine blessing, expressing the mercy of the Father, is described in the simple lines of Horatius Bonar:

> Upon a life I did not live,
> Upon a death I did not die,
> Another's life, Another's death,
> I stake my whole eternity.

Jesus lived a beautiful life when He was on earth. For thirty-plus years His thoughts, words, and actions were holy. He never sinned inwardly or outwardly. Everything that He thought about, said to others, and did was an expression of His perfect obedience. When He went to the cross to pay the penalty for our sins, He went there as the perfect Priest who offered up His perfect life as a sacrifice to satisfy divine justice.

But His perfect life had another benefit for us, and that is because He was not our representative only when He was on the cross. He was also our representative as He lived His perfect life, doing for us what we could not do for ourselves and providing for us a life that can be reckoned as ours before the omniscient eye of the Father. As Paul says in Romans 5:18–19, even as Adam by His disobedience brought us into condemnation, so by the obedience of Jesus many will be made righteous. How we should praise the Father for declaring us to be righteous, justified by faith in Jesus!

It is good to remind ourselves that justification is God's free gift to those who believe in Jesus. At the time he believes, especially if he has not had a Christian upbringing, a person may be unaware of all that is happening to him in the courts of heaven. But at that moment, he is justified by His merciful Father in heaven and is accepted in the Beloved (Eph. 1:6).

Adoption into God's Family

It is marvelous to understand that a sinner, when she believes in Jesus, is freely given by the merciful Father the permanent status of justification. But that blessing, great though it is, is not the only blessing the merciful Father gives because following justification, He also adopts that sinner into His family and she becomes an heir of God and a joint heir with Christ. Paul describes that status here when he says that believers "become heirs according to the hope of eternal life."

The inheritance they will have with Jesus is the experience of eternal life. While they enjoy eternal life now as a consequence of believing in Jesus, the full experience of eternal life is in the future after Jesus returns. After the resurrection, they will be glorified, fully like Jesus, a state described beautifully by the apostle John: "Beloved, now we are children of God; and it has not yet been revealed what we shall be, but we know that when He is revealed, we shall be like Him, for we shall see Him as He is" (1 John 3:2).

Paul writes in Romans 8:18–23 about how the whole creation will be set free from its state of bondage to the curse God imposed on it when Adam fell. He also says that the creation is groaning in the sense that it is anticipating the full redemption of the sons of God because that will be when it will be liberated. In ways that we cannot yet describe, the restored creation will be the inheritance Jesus will share with His people—and all because of the mercy of the Father.

What can we say to the Father in response? Surely, expressions of gratitude and thankfulness, whether in prayer or in praise.

14

Devotion, Divisiveness, and Dedicated Disciples

TITUS 3:8–15

---

8 *This is a faithful saying, and these things I want you to affirm*
constantly, that those who have believed in God should be careful to
maintain good works. These things are good and profitable to men.
9 *But avoid foolish disputes, genealogies, contentions, and striv-*
ings about the law; for they are unprofitable and useless. 10 *Reject a*
divisive man after the first and second admonition, 11 *knowing that*
such a person is warped and sinning, being self-condemned.
12 *When I send Artemas to you, or Tychicus, be diligent to come to*
me at Nicopolis, for I have decided to spend the winter there. 13 *Send*
Zenas the lawyer and Apollos on their journey with haste, that
they may lack nothing. 14 *And let our people also learn to maintain*
good works, to meet urgent needs, that they may not be unfruitful.
15 *All who are with me greet you. Greet those who love us in the*
faith. Grace be with you all. Amen.

Paul concludes his letter to Titus by repeating and enlarging on some matters he has already mentioned and then providing him with information about future plans. We can see that Paul is still strongly emphasizing good works, another reminder about his concern that the Cretan Christians must have a credible witness in their society.

Maintain Good Works

The apostle uses this phrase in verses 8 and 14 as he reminds Titus of the importance of this aspect of the believers' behavior. Possibly

Paul anticipated some objections to what he had written in the previous verses when he tells Titus that he has to insist the believers on Crete practice good works. Maybe he was concerned that there would be objections to acknowledging the authority of the government or to engaging gently and respectfully with unbelievers.

His descriptions of good works indicate that believers must focus on such behavior. In verse 8, the believers have to be careful to do them continually, which points to watchfulness about them; and in verse 14, the believers have to learn to do them, which indicates that there had to be diligence in performing them. The necessity for watchfulness and diligence is shown by Paul's drawing attention to cases of urgent need that should be dealt with. The outcome of such watchfulness and diligence is much to be desired. Paul describes the effects as excellent and profitable as well as fruitful.

What causes the outcome of good works? In verse 8, when Paul refers to the faithful saying, he is pointing back to what he wrote in verses 4–7, which is a beautiful summary of the gospel. The gospel is the motivation for all aspects of dedicated service, including expressions of good works. It is not hard to imagine that the Cretans would have learned that summary by heart (as well as the summary in 2:11–14) and reflected on what is said in it about the contents of the gospel. And it is also the case that Paul follows both statements with a command to Titus that he include the gospel when he teaches about Christian living.

Divisive Dangers

Paul then reminds Titus that he should "avoid foolish disputes, genealogies, contentions, and strivings about the law," which he already referred to in chapter 1:10–16 when he gave a warning about the Jewish teachers who were disturbing the churches in Crete with empty ideas. Avoiding includes a determined choice, a refusal to participate in, listen to, or discuss these notions. There could be a temptation to attempt winning an argument about possible meanings of biblical references, but such attempts would be profitless. Avoiding is a straightforward thing to do. All that is required is to walk away.

What the apostle says about wrong ideas also applies to the person who is advocating them. In words that refer to the authority that he reminded Titus of at the close of chapter 2, Paul requires Titus to warn such an individual regarding his actions. Titus can even warn him twice, but after that, if the person does not listen, Titus is to have no contact with him. The divisive person has no desire to submit his mind to the truth of God; his actions and words condemn him.

Paul does not indicate why Titus should avoid the divisive person. Perhaps the reasons are obvious. If Titus continued to interact with the man, it could give the impression that the man had something worthwhile to say. Titus was to be an example in not showing any interest in false doctrine. The members of the churches would see that false doctrine should be of no interest to them.

Dedicated Disciples

Paul mentions four believers in the closing verses. Artemas is not mentioned elsewhere in the New Testament. Tychicus is mentioned on several occasions. He accompanied Paul on his journey to Jerusalem to deliver the collection he had gathered (Acts 20:4); he delivered the letters that Paul sent to Ephesus and Colosse (Eph. 6:21; Col. 4:7); he may have come to Crete at Paul's bidding (Titus 3:12); and later on, Paul sent him to Ephesus (2 Tim. 4:12). Tychicus was a person on whom Paul could rely, and maybe he fulfilled roles that were similar to those of Titus. Paul, when writing to the Colossians, calls Tychicus "a beloved brother, faithful minister, and fellow servant in the Lord" (Col. 4:7). When Tychicus reached Colosse, he would be a comforter of the believers there (v. 8). Such a man would have been suitable in Crete, and since Paul was not sure whether he would send Tychicus or Artemas to Crete, we can be sure that Artemas was equally qualified.

The other two believers are Zenas the lawyer and Apollos. Maybe they had delivered this letter to Titus on their way to another location. They were definitely coming to Crete, and Titus was to help them move on to their next destination. Paul may even be suggesting in verse 14 that a good work the believers could engage in was to help in the mission of Zenas and Apollos by providing for their needs.

This is the only mention of Zenas in the New Testament, whereas Apollos is mentioned several times. He was an Alexandrian Jew who had been influenced by John the Baptist but was deficient in his knowledge of Jesus. On coming to Ephesus, he was helped in his understanding by Priscilla and Aquila to such an extent that the church there was happy to commend him to the church in Corinth. He was an eloquent speaker, yet humble and willing to learn from others. He knew how to defend the faith against Jewish opponents (Acts 18:24–19:1). It is not surprising that some in Corinth identified him as a potential leader, an attitude that was condemned by Paul (1 Cor. 3:1–4:6).

As we consider the information that Paul provides, we can see his care for the churches, exhibited by his sending gifted men to different churches and countries. We can also sense something of the effort and travel that such men engaged in in order to serve the Savior and His people. Most of what they did is unknown to us, but it is recorded in heaven. Moreover, we can see how dependent they were on the help of Christians as they traveled. While in the Western world we may not encounter individuals who serve in this way, there are other parts of the world where ministry is provided by traveling preachers visiting small communities of believers and providing them with instruction from God's Word, and they in turn provide for the practical needs of the preachers.

Paul's Closing Greetings

Paul informs Titus that those with him, wherever he is, are sending greetings. No information is given as to whether they have met Titus previously. Moreover, Paul asks Titus to pass on greetings to the believers in Crete, and while many of them had met Paul, they probably had not met those with him because the churches in Crete had not been in existence for long.

What was the point of these greetings? They were simple expressions of brotherly love by Paul and those with him. The salutations were evidence that God had renewed their hearts and created within them a deep interest in the progress of the gospel in other places. It is likely that their greetings were stimulated by the prayerful interest they had in the affairs of the people of God in Crete. Who can estimate the effect on the Cretans to hear that their founder had not forgotten them and that others far away were interested in them? It was very unlikely that the greetings were a casual hello. More likely, their thoughts are summarized in Paul's closing words, "Grace be with you all." There we can see that he has not limited his greetings only to Titus but has sent them to all the believers with him on Crete.

Paul's closing provides a beautiful summary of the believers living on the island of Crete. He says that they "love us in the faith." People love one another for various reasons—they experience family love, the love of friendship, and the love connected to one's homeland. But the love that springs from belonging to the faith is very different because it is supernatural, the product of divine grace at work in the lives of sinners, created by and developed in them by the Holy Spirit.

The apostle's final sentence, "Grace be with you all," summarizes the desires of his heart. These words state his confidence in God that He will be with His people in a gracious manner. After all, "grace" is often another word for the particular manner of the presence of God at work in and through His people. And given that it is His sovereign grace, this greeting was a word of comfort and assurance for Titus that his God would give him great success in his efforts for the fledgling churches on Crete.

Philemon

Introduction to Philemon

Thirteen of Paul's letters are included in the New Testament. In some of them, he refers to other letters he wrote but we no longer have, such as the letter to the Laodiceans that he mentions in Colossians 4:16 and the letters to the church in Corinth that he mentions in 1 Corinthians 5:9 and, probably, in 2 Corinthians 2:4. The background to twelve of Paul's New Testament letters includes problems that the churches faced, including the letters to Timothy and Titus, which were written to individuals functioning as apostolic delegates. Different from them all is his letter to Philemon, which basically concerns a domestic matter involving a man named Onesimus. He was a slave who had run away from his master Philemon but who had become a Christian through encountering Paul while he was imprisoned.

Paul probably wrote this short letter to Philemon during his first Roman imprisonment, around the time that he wrote the letter to the church in Colosse, if not at the same time. Several names—Timothy, Epaphras, Aristarchus, Mark, Luke, and Demas—appear in both letters, which reveals that they were composed when those people were with Paul. Yet there are some differences in their circumstances. For example, in Colossians Aristarchus is described as a prisoner but not so in Philemon, whereas Epaphras is a prisoner in Philemon but not so described in Colossians, which could suggest that the letters were written at different times during those imprisonments.

Onesimus is mentioned in Colossians 4:7–9 as accompanying Tychicus on his visit to Colosse to deliver the letter to the Colossians. It has been suggested that this indicates Onesimus was now engaged in serving with Paul because he had already received Philemon's approval for that, which the apostle may have requested in his letter to him. If that suggestion is correct, it would mean that the letter to Philemon preceded the one to the Colossians. It may be the case, however, that this visit by Onesimus was the same as the one mentioned in Philemon. Yet if that was the case, it is surprising that Tychicus is not mentioned as delivering the letter to Philemon.

It is not necessary for us to know the precise relationships these letters have to one another in order to appreciate the importance of the brief letter to Philemon. Although short, it deals with ongoing weighty matters such as the nature of Christian forgiveness, the necessity of prayer, the leadership style of the apostle Paul, and the provision of hospitality for traveling preachers. It also has something to say about the first-century Christian response to the form of slavery that existed in the Roman Empire.

Colosse (along with the neighboring cities of Laodicea and Hierapolis), which was about 120 miles east of Ephesus, was badly damaged, if not destroyed, by a major earthquake about AD 61. This suggests that Paul wrote both letters before the earthquake, as it would have taken some time to rebuild those cities, and such a date would also explain why he makes no mention of that disaster in his letters to the Colossians and to Philemon.

15

Saying a Lot in a Few Words

PHILEMON 1–3

---

1 *Paul, a prisoner of Christ Jesus, and Timothy our brother,*
To Philemon our beloved friend and fellow laborer, 2 *to the*
beloved Apphia, Archippus our fellow soldier, and the church in
your house:
3 *Grace to you and peace from God our Father and the Lord*
Jesus Christ.

How much can a person say in a few words? We could ask that question about several areas of life. Yet I want us to think of the statement at the beginning of this letter and ask this question. Perhaps we might think initially that we would find more important matters in some other verses in the Bible than in these. For example, we could think of John 3:16, which is a well-known verse describing how God procured salvation for His people through the gospel. But what can we find in the opening three verses of Philemon? In order to help us do so, we can divide it into three points: the senders of the letter, the recipients of the letter, and the blessing that the senders mention.

The Senders

As we can see, the senders are Paul and Timothy, although a quick read of the letter indicates that primarily the sender is Paul. Yet since Paul and Timothy are linked in this way, we can ask what we know about their relationship. We know that Timothy became a colleague of Paul during his second missionary journey when he revisited locations in Asia Minor, including Lystra, where Timothy lived (Acts 16:1–3). So the senders were servants of Jesus.

They served together, although neither of them was well physically. Paul said that Timothy had frequent infirmities (1 Tim. 5:23), and he also refers to several of his own health issues, such as his poor eyesight (Gal. 4:15) and his thorn in the flesh (2 Cor. 12:7). Clearly, these men did not regard their health concerns as reasons for not serving Jesus.

There was quite a difference in their respective ages, with Timothy perhaps more than twenty years younger than Paul. Indeed, Timothy initially had served as a kind of apprentice to Paul and worked with him in a manner similar to how a son would work with his father, learning the family trade. Their difference in age did not prevent them working together for Jesus.

If we were to limit the descriptions of each of them to one feature, what would we identify? When Paul says that he is "a prisoner of Christ Jesus," he is showing us how to think about adverse providences. Paul did not know the full picture of why the Lord had allowed him to be arrested when he was in Jerusalem delivering a collection, which then brought about one link after another in the chain of his life (Acts 21–28). But "of Christ Jesus" gives us the key for understanding Paul's self-assessment. He knew that all of life, even situations of adversity, were designed for him by God in order for him to serve Jesus. Therefore, Paul was able to have a right focus. And we know that in prison he had served the Lord in writing letters to churches, in witnessing to his guards, and in encouraging his friends (Phil. 1:12–18). Paul's self-description is a reminder of his priority and a challenge to us regarding how to view life. Do we see our current circumstances as being primarily for Christ?

When Paul describes Timothy as "our brother," he is highlighting the amazing doctrine of adoption. Although he had been brought up well by his mother and grandmother (2 Tim. 1:5), Timothy was not a Christian when he was born. There had to be a moment when he repented of his sins and embraced Jesus as his Savior. Many blessings came to him as a result, such as the forgiveness of all his sins. Another of those blessings was that he became a member of the family of God and a fellow heir with Jesus, as all believers in Jesus experience (Rom. 8:17). To be so elevated is a wonderful privilege and an appropriate way to consider God's amazing grace. He takes His people from a low condition, as rebels against Him, and places them in a high condition, as full members of His family, a membership that is eternal.

So we learn from this brief self-description that it is important for servants of Jesus to have a right understanding of divine providence and a correct awareness of the doctrine of adoption into God's family.

The Recipients

It is likely that Paul is writing to a Christian family living in Colosse. Philemon and Apphia are husband and wife, and Archippus is their son. Philemon was a wealthy man; he owned at least one slave (Onesimus), and his house was large enough to host church meetings. Yet Paul does not address them according to their social status. Instead, he refers to them in ways that highlight their Christian living.

There was obviously a warm and affectionate bond between Paul (and Timothy) and Philemon. It could be the case that God used Paul to bring Philemon to faith at some time in the past (v. 16). So it is not surprising that Paul calls him "beloved." In addition, Paul refers to him as a "fellow laborer," although they were currently miles apart and living in very different circumstances. Paul was imprisoned, and Philemon was in his house in Colosse.

When we think of a worker, at least two ideas come to mind: (1) at what is that person working, and (2) for whom is he or she working? As far as Paul and Philemon were concerned, in a spiritual sense they were working at strengthening the church in whatever ways they could. An example would be that Paul worked at helping the church by writing letters, and Philemon contributed to the church by holding services in his house (the "your" before "house" is singular). Both activities could be arduous. They were helped and motived to participate in this work because they realized that they were working for the Head of the church, Jesus.

Apphia was likely mentioned among the three recipients because she was Philemon's wife. (It is possible that she was his sister and that Archippus was another brother.) She is mentioned as sharing a privileged position as a member of the family of God, which made her equal with every member of that family as far as status was concerned.

Archippus is described as a "fellow soldier," a reminder that there is a spiritual war taking place between the kingdom of light and the kingdom of darkness. All Christians are involved in this battle unless they are showing cowardice. When Paul wrote this letter, he was probably in the presence of a soldier who was guarding him carefully. The apostle could tell if that soldier relaxed from his responsibility. He wanted Archippus to remind himself that he was engaged in a daily battle with the enemies of Jesus. Spiritual warfare is a big theme in the Bible and is an activity in which all Christians are engaged from their conversion to the end of their life.

There are two other observations to be made. First, it is worth noting when reading Paul's letters that he says something commendable about Christians to whom he writes. That is a good example for us to follow. Second, here is an example of a family happily serving the Lord together. Often, we are told in the New Testament, especially in Acts, of how a person's household also believed the gospel. We have no idea which of the three was the first to become a Christian, but we can see that each of them did.

In passing, Paul also mentions the church that met in Philemon's home. After the Lord opened the heart of Philemon to the gospel, evidence of his new life was that he put his assets at the disposal of the Lord to use for the benefit of His kingdom. Every Lord's Day, and perhaps at other times as well, believers gathered at his home for worship and fellowship. They were the church in Colosse as well as the church in Philemon's house. The word "church" signified people and not a building, people involved with one another because of the gospel.

So we can see from the description of the recipients the importance of realizing that Christians are working together for the Lord, that He has given them a wonderful status, that they are engaged in spiritual battles, and that they should use their assets for the benefit of the kingdom.

The Blessing

Paul's greeting is similar to greetings found in his other letters. His frequent use of it raises the question of why he did so. An answer George Muller gives is likely the case: "We have to be reminded that grace has been bestowed upon us by God through Christ Jesus, and that he is willing to bestow more and more blessing."[1] This is a simple explanation and wonderful to experience!

There is no doubt that Paul earnestly desired that his beloved friends would experience the blessings of grace and peace. But he knew that he himself, despite his position in the church as an apostle, did not have the power or ability to give this blessing to other believers. Therefore, his greeting is not an expression of his competence but of his awareness of the competence of the Father and Jesus.

What is grace? It is the totality of all saving blessings. A person who would attempt to describe it would run out of words. It means the fullness of divine favor to God's people. When speaking about it, we can safely place it alongside other salvation words. We have electing grace, redeeming grace, justifying grace, adopting grace, sanctifying grace, and glorifying grace. God shows His grace in providence, in answering our prayers, in protecting us from danger, in fulfilling His promises, in pardoning our sins, in giving us spiritual victories, and in correcting us. In what area of life will it not be at work through the activities of the Spirit? Grace is God acting for us at all times in order to bring spiritual blessings to us.

The particular effect of grace Paul mentions is peace. He is not referring to having peace with God in the sense that He and His

---

1. George Muller, "Paul's Letter to Philemon," in *Jehovah Magnified: Addresses* (Bristol: W. Mack, 1876), 184.

people are reconciled when they believe in Jesus and become His people. Rather, he is describing the inner experience of peace, part of the fruit of the Spirit that Paul lists in Galatians 5:22–23.

It is easy to assume that another reason Paul used this form of blessing was his own experience of grace and peace. He had on many occasions of difficulty found that the answer to all those situations was the grace and peace that came to him from heaven. Under the guidance of the Holy Spirit, the words flowed into his letters on numerous occasions because the blessings had flowed into his heart on numerous occasions. His greeting is a reminder of the riches of divine grace available to us.

The apostle probably realized that Philemon would need divine grace to fulfill the request in the letter about Onesimus. After all, it would involve Philemon forgiving Onesimus for whatever harm he had caused. Moreover, Paul was asking Philemon to do something that was countercultural in a sense. In life, a slave could be set free as an expression of gratitude for a worthy action. But Philemon was asked to do something that most people in Colosse would never have seen before—grant forgiveness and freedom. What would enable Philemon to do so? Grace. And what would be the outcome? Peace.

Since Paul had used this form of blessing numerous times, we can see in his practice a desire to be careful when referring to the actions of the divine persons. It is because God is their Father that He can give such blessings to them. Grace here is family grace that issues in peace, an experience that cannot be known by sinners until they become members of the family of God. And grace and peace are given because Jesus is the appointed Mediator, the one who provides His people with blessing from the heavenly throne because He is their Prophet, Priest, and King, instructing them, helping them, and defending them.

Surely Philemon would have been encouraged by this salutation to give the response that Paul wanted. We can imagine the peace that would have come into his heart once he had done so. This is a powerful challenge to us when God asks us to do something that initially seems difficult. Obedience is enabled by grace and rewarded with peace from heaven. It is also a powerful challenge to us when God asks us to do something that seems straightforward. We will need grace to do it. Such grace is available, and the outcome will be peace.

16

Paul's Prayer for Philemon

PHILEMON 4–7

---

[4]I thank my God, making mention of you always in my prayers, [5]hearing of your love and faith which you have toward the Lord Jesus and toward all the saints, [6]that the sharing of your faith may become effective by the acknowledgment of every good thing which is in you in Christ Jesus. [7]For we have great joy and consolation in your love, because the hearts of the saints have been refreshed by you, brother.

A book of prayers can be helpful to believers for a variety of reasons. Recently, I read a book of prayers by John Knox, and now I can to some extent appreciate why his prayers had such an effect on those who heard them, including his opponents and even monarchs. I have also appreciated reading the prayers of C. H. Spurgeon, which were transcribed at the time. In using such books, we can learn from how these individuals prayed. We see how they addressed God, what biblical arguments they used when pleading with God, how they used biblical doctrines as they prayed, or what they said to the Lord when praying in times of puzzling providences in their lives.

In addition to books containing prayers, we can read about occasions of prayer in Christian biography. Such books can describe the use of prayer in the lives of Christians in a variety of circumstances. Often, the authors recount prayers for guidance, intercession for others, pleas for personal spiritual revival, longings stated to God about spiritual recovery of his cause, or desires for closer fellowship with him that were experienced by the subjects of the biographies.

In the Bible there are numerous examples of prayers in the book of Psalms as well as occasional prayers elsewhere in the Old Testament by individuals like Abraham, Daniel, and Nehemiah, who teach us how to pray in a variety of circumstances. In the New Testament is the Lord's Prayer, some recorded prayers in the book of Acts, and Paul's prayers in his letters. Such prayers reveal to us the spirit of prayer that prevails with God as well as the contents of biblical prayer.

Prayer says a great deal about a person. One of my elders in a former congregation prayed daily for every home in the community, mentioning each person to the Lord. The number amounted to several hundred people every day. I'm sure he prayed for others as well. His example informed me that Paul's patterns and methods of prayer can be attained by others. With the Lord's enablement, all it takes is time and dedication.

This may be only a subtle difference, but Paul does not say here that he remembers to pray for Philemon but that he remembers Philemon in his prayers. How do we remember a person? It usually involves some consideration of them, recalling features of their lives and circumstances. Remembering a person before God is quite a bit different from merely mentioning a person to God.

I suppose many a person has wished that he or she could pray like Paul. But how to do so is the problem. Yet we can start by observing when and why and how he prayed. We can note the different features in each of his recorded prayers as well as the features that may be common to all of them. So what can we find in his prayer for Philemon?

Prayer Requires a Relationship with God

Sometimes a pronoun makes all the difference. Paul could have written in verse 4 that he thanked God when he prayed for Philemon, and obviously that would be a true statement. Yet his use of the pronoun "my" brings a different emphasis to his prayers. What can we derive about Paul from his use of "my God"?

First, it is a sign that Paul was converted. Most people know something about the apostle's conversion because the phrase "a Damascus experience" has become common parlance. That phrase may be used to highlight the suddenness of a person's change of mind. In Paul's case, while it was sudden, it was also genuine. He had become a new creature by becoming a disciple of Jesus. When the Lord sent Ananias a short time later to speak to Paul, He indicated to Ananias that Paul's conversion was genuine because Paul was praying (Acts 9:11). From one point of view, that description is surprising because Paul would have prayed often as a Pharisee. But he had never prayed to God as His child until he was converted.

Second, the pronoun "my" indicates that Paul realized he was in a covenant relationship with God. Such an idea is normal in the Bible and is expressed in many ways, such as when someone says God is his portion, or God is his defender or his refuge. When Paul met Jesus on the road to Damascus, it was the onset of a life of discovering the resources available for him in God. He knew that he could talk to his God at any time, and God allowed him to bring freely to Him all burdens and concerns, as well as all other matters that were appropriate. And among them was his prayers for churches and for individuals such as Philemon.

Third, the pronoun "my" testifies to Paul's experience of divine grace, that over the years he had received many answers to his prayers from his God and Father. The heavenly Father had given to the apostle abundant reasons to have confidence that he was a member of the divine family, realizing in numerous ways the riches of divine grace. When Paul was converted, he entered into a covenant relationship that brought great blessings into his experience, and many of them he received in answer to prayer.

Prayer Requires Relevant Information

Paul knew some details about Philemon's life because he writes that he was aware "of your love and faith which you have toward the

Lord Jesus and toward all the saints." The apostle uses the present tense here, suggesting that he is being told constantly about Philemon. Who would have provided this information? Onesimus, now that he is converted, would have told Paul about how Philemon lived. Another source of this information would have been Epaphras, whom Paul mentions is with him and who was from Colosse. Indeed, we are told in Colossians that he brought the gospel to Colosse initially (Col. 1:7). It is likely that Philemon would have helped Epaphras as he worked for God there.

We can imagine Paul and Epaphras and Onesimus speaking together. The apostle would hear things about life in the church in Colosse. Among the details he received would have been a commendation of the way Philemon was living. And there is no doubt that Paul would have turned those details into definite prayer points concerning Philemon.

This is a reminder that Paul must have spent a great deal of time in prayer. We can see this is the case from the way he describes his prayer life in his letters. While it is possible to assume that he did this because he was a pastor, we should also remember that he tells Christians that they should pray without ceasing (1 Thess. 5:17) and they should pray continually (Col. 4:2). Such praying is presented in the New Testament as normal for Christians.

Perhaps you have heard the story of two ministers who were discussing the text about praying without ceasing and wondering what it meant because they found it difficult to practice. A maid who overhead them told them that she found it straightforward. They asked her how that could be. She replied that when she got dressed, she prayed that God would clothe her with Christ's righteousness; that when she was eating, she prayed that her soul would feed on the bread of life; that when she was walking, she prayed that she would walk in the paths of righteousness. She could pray relevantly in every circumstance she was in. The ministers realized that she did indeed understand the thrust of the text.

Paul says something unsurprising and something unusual about Philemon's behavior. It is unsurprising that he possessed love and faith toward Jesus and showed love to the saints.[1] But what does Paul mean when he says that Philemon expressed faith toward his fellow believers in Colosse?

In his devotional explanation of this brief letter, George Müller suggested that Paul means that Philemon was "looking upon them with faith, seeing in them that they are the children of God, treating them as such, as the children of God. Whenever we are able to look on one another as the children of God, whenever we are enabled to see Christ in one another, that is exercising faith towards one another."[2] We see here a beautiful expression of brotherly love by Philemon when he trusted those he helped to behave as children of God not to abuse his kindnesses for them.

Prayer for Christians Focuses on Growth in Grace

Paul informed Philemon about the goals he has in his prayers for him: "that the sharing of your faith may become effective by the acknowledgment of every good thing which is in you in Christ Jesus."

In this statement, Paul says three things about Philemon's actions. First, his faith needs to be effective. Second, effectiveness will occur when what Paul calls "the acknowledgment of every good thing that is in you" happens. Third, it all happens for the sake of Christ.

When we consider the necessity of effectiveness, it is a reminder that Philemon's actions in themselves were not the goal. Whatever those actions were, there also had to be spiritual benefits. How would those benefits be achieved? By prayer. So whether the action

---

1. Some scholars suggest that Paul's grammatical method indicates that he meant faith in the Lord Jesus and love to all the saints. This grammatical explanation involves Paul's using a chiastic structure when he refers to love and faith, and this structure shows that "love" refers to the saints, and "faith" refers to Christ. This may be the case, and if so, then we can see two clear features of Philemon's life for which Paul is grateful—his faith in Christ and his love for the saints. Yet it is possible to see how a believer could have faith in other Christians with whom he or she is involved.

2. George Müller, "Paul's Letter to Philemon," in *Jehovah Magnified: Addresses* (Bristol: W. Mack, 1876), 186.

was occasional or consistent, it had to be accompanied by and followed up with prayer. And not just by the prayers of Philemon. Others, like Paul, had to be involved by prayer, which is a reminder of the importance of shared information.

Then there is Paul's desire for experiencing "every good thing which is in you," because by "acknowledgment" he means experience. The good things that are within God's people are the things that His grace has put there. They cover a wide range of possibilities, and when they are used, they bring blessings to others and prayer is answered.

For example, we could consider Philemon's desire to use his home as a place for the church to meet. That inner desire was in him because of divine grace. In his case, it led him to share joyfully his possessions with those he now loved. When the church came together, they would receive blessings from God, which would not have occurred if Philemon had not shared what he had. So others experienced divine blessing within them as they saw God's hand in the provision and when they met with those whom divine love had caused them to embrace. Maybe others in the community saw what was going on between Philemon and the other Christians there and they wondered what caused them to behave like that. Perhaps with time they would also become Christians. So the blessings of Christ would spread to more and more people.

What are the reason and the goal for all such actions? Paul tells us that they take place for Christ. Believers should do what they do because they love Jesus. That becomes the paramount aim for anything. In reality, all that they do should come under the umbrella of serving Christ. But here Paul is describing the relationships between believers and how they should aim to do all for Christ as they interact with one another.

When we think of the main purpose of the letter, we can ask how this focus in Paul's prayer is connected to it. The purpose was for Philemon to forgive Onesimus and set him free from being a slave so that he could serve Christ alongside Paul. If Philemon did so, people would see the effectiveness of Paul's prayer for this to happen, the good thing of forgiveness in Philemon's heart, and how he wanted to set Onesimus free in order for him to serve Christ.

Prayer Often Flows from Rejoicing

Paul wants to encourage Philemon and does so by stating the effects on him of his friend's reported actions. He says that "we have great joy and consolation in your love, because the hearts of the saints have been refreshed by you, brother." It is evident from these words that Paul had a warm heart for all the people of God, including those in Colosse whom he had never met, and longed for them to experience the benefits of grace through divinely given mutual love in action.

An important aspect of the Christian life is the pleasure we give to other Christians. This pleasure is always connected to our showing evidence of divine grace at work in our lives. Philemon gave delight to Paul because of the refreshment the believers in Colosse enjoyed through his activities. The word translated "refreshed" was sometimes used to describe the period of rest that an army enjoyed between marches. An obvious application is that the Christians in Colosse obtained spiritual rest from daily spiritual conflict when they met in Philemon's house on the Lord's Day.

Philemon could have helped needy believers in many other ways. But his actions for them made it easy for Paul to pray for him that he would increase in such activities and continue to meet the deep inner needs of his fellow Christians. It is not surprising that Paul delighted to pray for Philemon. And here is a real challenge for us: each of us can ask, How does my life influence the prayer requests of other believers when I come to their minds?

17

The Conversion of Onesimus

PHILEMON 8–16

[8]Therefore, though I might be very bold in Christ to command you what is fitting, [9]yet for love's sake I rather appeal to you—being such a one as Paul, the aged, and now also a prisoner of Jesus Christ—[10]I appeal to you for my son Onesimus, whom I have begotten while in my chains, [11]who once was unprofitable to you, but now is profitable to you and to me.

[12]I am sending him back. You therefore receive him, that is, my own heart, [13]whom I wished to keep with me, that on your behalf he might minister to me in my chains for the gospel. [14]But without your consent I wanted to do nothing, that your good deed might not be by compulsion, as it were, but voluntary.

[15]For perhaps he departed for a while for this purpose, that you might receive him forever, [16]no longer as a slave but more than a slave—a beloved brother, especially to me but how much more to you, both in the flesh and in the Lord.

Our daily experience is often routine. No doubt, that was the case with Philemon most of the time. He would have had happy days and surprising days and also disappointing days. One of the disappointing days would have been when his slave Onesimus ran away. Philemon would not have known where Onesimus had gone, and he may not have known why his slave had run away. If Onesimus had fled because of a misdemeanor, eventually Philemon would have found out. But he would not expect to see Onesimus again in his house. Then this letter from Paul arrives, and what may have seemed to be a routine day became surprising and happy in Philemon's household. Imagine how the news spread around that Christian household—Onesimus had become a Christian!

Unexpected Conversions

There have been many surprising conversions to Jesus Christ. Some are mentioned in the New Testament—we can think of the tax collector Matthew or the thief on the cross or Saul of Tarsus as examples—and others are mentioned in Christian biographies and elsewhere. Among them is the conversion of the runaway slave Onesimus.

Onesimus had chosen to leave Philemon's household and somehow made his way to Rome, which was several hundred miles away, probably to hide among its vast population. Perhaps eventually he had been arrested there for a petty offense and found himself imprisoned. We are not told how he came to be there, yet there he had been converted through the influence of Paul, who was now sending him back to his master, whom we assume would not have expected a letter containing such wonderful news. How had this come about?

Onesimus and Philemon's Prayers

To begin with, I would suggest that Philemon had prayed for Onesimus many times before he ran away. Philemon was a good and kind master, and in addition he was a Christian master who would desire intensely spiritual blessings for his entire household, including his slaves. Therefore, it is very likely that he prayed regularly for Onesimus's conversion.

We don't know what Philemon's reaction was to Onesimus's flight, and neither did Paul, which explains his earnest plea to Philemon to treat Onesimus in a Christian manner. Probably Philemon was disappointed by what Onesimus had done, but that should not have been a reason for assuming that God had ignored his prayers. The Lord often chooses very unexpected—indeed, unusual—ways to answer our prayers.

Onesimus and Divine Providence

The next detail that covers the experience of Onesimus is divine providence. Sometimes we can speak about providence in a manner that suggests God acts only in response to our actions. Yet in reality divine providence is the outworking of God's eternal plan and His total control over everything that occurs. We can put it this way: from Philemon's perspective, Onesimus seemed to be running away from the ways of God; from God's perspective, Onesimus was running toward his meeting with God, although that would not have been how Onesimus would have seen it before the meeting took place.

There are many aspects connected to God's implementation of His eternal plan that are hard to understand, especially with regard to how humans' sinful actions are included in it. Onesimus was wrong to run away from his good master. As a slave in that culture, he had responsibilities to fulfill, and it was an expression of disobedience for him to rebel. Yet in ways that we cannot grasp, Onesimus's actions, although wrong, were both included in God's plan and under His sovereign control.

This reality is basic to the Christian faith. Peter informed his audience on the day of Pentecost that while Jesus was "delivered by the determined purpose and foreknowledge of God," He was "taken by lawless hands…crucified, and put to death" (Acts 2:23). The apostle fearlessly declared that the sin of crucifying Jesus was included in God's plan and that his listeners were also responsible for bringing it about. Paul himself knew that he had been chosen by God and that the Lord had also predetermined the time of his conversion, which took place while he was rushing to Damascus to punish sinfully the followers of Jesus there.

How can people respond to this reality? Some will hate it because they imagine it undermines their freedom. Yet they had no control over the day of their birth, and they have no power to bring about with certainty anything that they plan. So they don't possess total freedom in any case. Yet we should not be surprised that some will hate the idea of a sovereign God who fulfills His own purpose.

Further, animosity is better than apathy in the sense that their hostility may lead them to try and outthink the doctrine, and in the process, they may be enlightened to see the truth. After all, many surprising conversions have come from among such people.

A second possible response is fatalism, the idea that says, "If I am going to be converted, I will be converted no matter what I do." Some even twist it further and say, "I may want to be converted, but if God has not put my name in His plan, I will still be lost." The problem with such people is that they are not listening to the Christian message, which says very clearly that the only way by which people can know if they are in the saving plan of God is by repenting of their sins and trusting in Jesus. Through the gospel they are invited to freely choose to believe in Jesus.

The right response for such people is to accept that God is in sovereign control and accept His free offer of mercy that He pronounces in the gospel. This is what Onesimus did. We are not told how he came in contact with Paul. Perhaps he heard that Epaphras, the pastor from Colosse, was with Paul and went there. Or he may have come across Christian slaves or freemen in Rome who mentioned Paul to him, and he may have wondered if this was the same Paul who had influenced Philemon a few years earlier. The one thing we do know is that God arranged in providence for Philemon to come in contact with Paul while he was imprisoned.

Onesimus and Divine Pardon

Paul was able to speak to Onesimus about the gospel and how he could be forgiven. We can imagine the apostle speaking patiently and lovingly to Onesimus. In his other writings at this time, such as Philippians, Paul mentions how he was able to bring the gospel to the soldiers who were guarding him (Phil. 1:12–14). And God also permitted him to bring the good news to Onesimus. One obvious deduction we can make is that there is not a place where the gospel cannot be communicated successfully. There, in his confinement, Paul was free to share the message of Jesus with whoever came his way.

What did Onesimus need to hear? He needed to hear that all his sins could be forgiven. Perhaps to begin with he was concerned with only how his earthly master would respond to the wrongs committed against him. But Paul would have told him that he had a lot more wrongs to worry about—the sins he had done against God. Those sins included all his wrong thoughts, wrong words, and wrong actions. Paul would have informed Onesimus that he was guilty of innumerable sins against his Creator, who had determined to punish eternally all who had sinned against Him.

But Paul would have informed him also of what God had done about the situation. With great delight, the apostle would have recounted the life and work of Jesus, beginning with His eternal existence in heaven, His incarnation, His holy life, His death as a propitiation on behalf of sinners, His resurrection, and His exaltation to the throne of God. The apostle would also have told Onesimus about how Jesus had sent him as His ambassador to tell everyone he met about the forgiveness that could be received from God because of what Jesus had accomplished for sinners.

As the details penetrated Onesimus's mind and heart, he would sense a change coming over him. He began to feel sorry for having committed his sins, and he wanted to respond by faith to the living Savior who had died on the cross and was now risen from the dead. We cannot say how long the process took; it could have been a matter of hours or weeks, but the moment came when he experienced the regenerating power of the Holy Spirit and became a new creature. Having trusted in Jesus, Onesimus was immediately and completely forgiven by God and adopted into His family.

Onesimus and God's Purpose for Him

Why did God save Onesimus from his sins? Several answers could be given to this question, but two can be found in the description Paul gives of Onesimus. First, Onesimus had become a fellow servant with Paul. We can see this emphasis in Paul's description of him as "profitable to you and to me" (v. 11). Obviously, Onesimus knew what it was like to be a servant. As a slave, he had obeyed whatever

Philemon had commanded him to do. Now he had another Master, and how could he show obedience to Him? First, he did so by submitting himself voluntarily to the apostle's requirements and, second, by his being willing to accept his position in providence as Philemon's slave. We could say that he obeyed God in church demands and in the role given him in society. Obedience to God's requirements is the best evidence of salvation. Such obedience is comprehensive and not selective, constant and not intermittent, and voluntary and not forced.

One aspect of this new commitment to Jesus was very challenging. Paul wanted Onesimus to go back to Philemon and tell him that he was now a different kind of bondslave. Obviously, this would be a huge step for Onesimus. Was he willing to confess Jesus where he had previously been a disobedient servant? It is straightforward to serve in a place where no one knows much about our past. But what about those who do know us and whom we have wronged at some stage in our lives?

Onesimus had done personal wrong to Philemon, and Paul knew it was appropriate that Onesimus and Philemon should be reconciled. The members of the church in Colosse needed to know if Philemon and Onesimus were reconciled, because if they were not, what should the church pray for regarding them? Perhaps the witness of the church in Colosse would be damaged if either of them failed to embrace the other because the failure would indicate that the gospel did not change sinners and make them like Jesus. Onesimus needed to know if Philemon would forgive him for his previous sinful behavior and wrongdoing; otherwise, he would carry the memory of his wrongdoing on his heart.

So one aspect of God's will for Onesimus was for him to live as a fellow servant with others of His servants. In addition, it was God's will that he should live as a brother with all who were in God's family. If the challenge for Onesimus was to go back to Colosse and seek reconciliation with Philemon, the challenge for Philemon was to treat the penitent Onesimus as a brother. Onesimus was probably not the first slave in Colosse to run away, but I suspect he was the first returned slave to be treated as a brother by his offended master!

Philemon was to treat Onesimus as a brother because they were both members of God's family. This does not mean that Philemon should have given liberty to Onesimus; Paul does not say to Philemon that he should not have slaves. It is impossible for us to know whether or not Paul personally believed that slavery would disappear before the second coming of Jesus. We cannot impose our cultural norms on an ancient culture that could not even imagine them. Instead, Paul is saying to Philemon that he should never forget Onesimus is now a member of God's family, and he should use what God has given him for Onesimus's benefit when he comes home.

We can read these references to slavery and assume that they have no relevance to us because slavery is not a problem we face. Yet to do so is to ignore Paul's basic principle here that social and cultural differences should not cause disunity and divisions among Christians. While Onesimus could remain a slave, Philemon could not treat him merely as a slave. It was Philemon's responsibility to act appropriately toward all his slaves, and Paul is not suggesting that Philemon show favoritism toward Onesimus at the expense of other slaves. Instead, what he is asking for is a change in Philemon's attitude toward Onesimus. Now Onesimus is his slave for a season but his brother forever. They have the same dignity as sons of God, they should have the same delight in the things of God, and they should engage in the same determination to serve Christ as Lord.

Paul uses a play on the meaning of Onesimus's name in verse 11. It means "profitable" or "useful." Clearly, before his conversion, Onesimus had been unprofitable and useless when he ran away. Now, since his conversion, he is doubly profitable and useful—to Paul in Rome and soon for Philemon in Colosse. A. K. MacMurchy writes, "Beforetime Onesimus was unworthy of his fine name; now he is doubly worthy of it. He is thoroughly changed; now he is a new creature in Christ Jesus. That makes all the difference, and what a difference! Whereas formerly he was unprofitable, now he is certified to be doubly profitable."[1]

So we can see from Onesimus's experience how amazing the grace of God is. He knows how to find His lost sheep, lead them to Himself, integrate them into His family, and enable them to serve Him. He can take them from the depths of sin and enable them to rejoice in the experience of His amazing grace.

---

1. A. K. MacMurchy, *The Epistle of Paul to Philemon: A Series of Expositions* (Edinburgh: Oliphant, Anderson and Ferrier, 1898), 89.

18

Paul, the Church Leader

PHILEMON 8–9, 21–22

---

[8]*Therefore, though I might be very bold in Christ to command you what is fitting,* [9]*yet for love's sake I rather appeal to you—being such a one as Paul, the aged, and now also a prisoner of Jesus Christ....*

[21]*Having confidence in your obedience, I write to you, knowing that you will do even more than I say.* [22]*But, meanwhile, also prepare a guest room for me, for I trust that through your prayers I shall be granted to you.*

It is possible to regard Paul's letter to Philemon as merely an example of a personal letter that Paul wrote to a friend in order to give some advice on a domestic issue. Yet while it is obviously a personal letter, it also has implications beyond the household of Philemon because it will affect the witness of the church in the community and even the future ministry of the apostle Paul, should Onesimus serve alongside him in some way.

So how would we expect Philemon to know what to do with this unexpected request from Paul? One contributing factor to his response would be his knowledge of Paul's leadership qualities, which would have revealed to him what kind of man Paul was. If Philemon knew that Paul had the right qualities, it would be easier to follow his instructions.

Obviously, we cannot know Paul from personal contact in the way that Philemon did. Yet we can deduce features of Paul's leadership in this letter he sent to Philemon. Indeed, we will see that this brief letter reveals several features that should mark leaders in the church of Jesus because they are features that He taught and modeled.

A Basic Feature

First, we will consider one important requirement for authentic leadership in the church before then observing seven beautiful leadership traits this letter shows Paul possessed.

Paul's basic concept of leadership is *servant leadership*. This aspect is seen in the title he gives to the Savior when he calls Him "the Lord Jesus Christ" (v. 3). No doubt Paul saw in this title the reality of the universal lordship of Jesus, the one who has been given all authority in heaven and on earth. Yet within that universal authority Paul would have also seen a particular authority, the authority that Jesus had over him as an individual Christian and as an individual church leader. Paul did not resent this authority; rather, he rejoiced in it. And seeing himself as a servant of Jesus enabled him to have a wide range of qualities in his service for his Master. Indeed, it is fair to say that all the other features of Paul's leadership cohere only because of this basic understanding that he was a servant of Jesus the Lord.

Paul knew that his personal way of serving Jesus was to do so as an apostle. Jesus had called him to this role that gave him great authority in the church. We see him exercising this authority in his various letters as he deals with wrong doctrines and practices that were present in the churches to which he wrote. Paul alludes to this authority when he says to Philemon that he could have commanded Philemon to obey him. Yet it is notable that he prefers not to command Philemon but to persuade him. This could have been a reason for Paul not mentioning his apostolic role in his greeting at the start of the letter, which he was accustomed to do in other letters.

This attitude of servant leadership should be the aim of all Christian leaders, and when it is kept in view, most of the problems linked mainly to inappropriate leadership behavior will not pester or inhibit Christian congregations.

Seven Beautiful Qualities

What qualities flow from servant leadership as described in this letter? The first is Paul's awareness that church leadership is *shared leadership*. In verse 1, he associates himself with Timothy. We are aware that Paul stresses this aspect of leadership in most of his letters. For example, when writing to the Thessalonians, he also mentions Silvanus and Timothy alongside himself (1 Thess. 1:1). In 1 Corinthians he links himself with Sosthenes, who was a leader in the assembly in Corinth (1 Cor. 1:1). Usually, it is Timothy whom he mentions.

The concept of shared leadership did not mean that Paul was not aware of his distinctive, authoritative position as an apostle and the responsibilities and privileges that accompanied it. As already noted, he alludes to them in verse 8 when he says that he was bold enough to command Philemon to obey him. But the apostle was also aware that sometimes using a strong, assertive manner was not the best way to proceed.

Nor did Paul's commitment to shared leadership indicate that he wanted to reduce his own involvement and ask others to do something because he did not wish to give 100 percent to his role. If that were the case, he could easily have asked Timothy to write a letter to Philemon. The strength of shared leadership is not that individuals can do less; rather, it is that shared leadership means more can get done for the kingdom as each leader uses his gifts to achieve the shared goal.

The obvious feature of shared leadership is harmony between the leaders. Paul himself knew the disastrous effects of disharmony in leadership that took place when he and Barnabas had their big disagreement that was so strong they had to separate (Acts 15:36–41). How is harmony between leaders achieved? What was it that brought about the harmony between Paul and Timothy? Obviously, at one level it happened because Paul was Timothy's mentor and Timothy served with Paul as a son would with a father. And it also existed because of Timothy's attitude, which Paul describes in a letter sent about the same time as this letter to Philemon. Writing to the Philippians, Paul, the pleased father, says of Timothy, "For I have no one like-minded, who will sincerely care for your state. For all seek their own, not the things which are of Christ Jesus. But you know his proven character, that as a son with his father he served with me in the gospel" (Phil. 2:20–22). What maintained the harmony and enabled shared leadership was the beautiful determination of Paul and Timothy to serve the interests of Jesus Christ. And that prior dedication is an essential element for harmonious and lasting church leadership.

The second quality of leadership that Paul shows is what can be called *submissive leadership*. What is in view here is Paul's submissive spirit to God's providence for him. Where is Paul at the time of writing? He is imprisoned, awaiting a verdict from the Roman authorities as to whether or not he will be set free. It is important to note that Paul did not assume his current circumstances were a reason for not continuing with his work as a leader. Instead, he noted what he could still do and did it.

It is amazing to observe what Paul accomplished for Jesus because of this attitude of submissive leadership. We know that during his imprisonment he wrote several letters of the New Testament (Ephesians, Philippians, Colossians, and Philemon). He also indicates in Philippians 1 that he managed to convey the gospel to the guards placed over him to such an extent that the reasons for his imprisonment were known throughout the palace. Moreover, that he was able to maintain his leadership roles encouraged other believers in Rome to fulfill their tasks.

Usually, our response to Paul's achievements is to assume that he was a kind of superman who possessed extraordinary gifts. Yet he tells us that he had a weak physical presence (2 Cor. 10:10), was not a good speaker (2 Cor. 11:6), and was sometimes afraid (1 Cor. 2:3). So how was he able to do so much? I would suggest it was because he recognized the sovereignty of Jesus as the arranger of his circumstances and expected to receive the strength from Him in order to fulfill his calling.

A third aspect of Paul's leadership can be called *supplicatory leadership*, by which I mean that all he did was surrounded by earnest prayer. It is obvious from Paul's letters, including this one to Philemon, that he did nothing without prayer. His prayers were not vague but focused and connected to what he knew about the current circumstances of those for whom he was praying. As far as Philemon was concerned, Paul's prayer was connected to what he had heard of Philemon's love and faith, and therefore the apostle prayed that the sharing of Philemon's faith would be effective (v. 6).

Paul did not stress only his own prayers. He wanted Philemon to pray for him, especially with regard to his desire that he would be able to visit Colosse. Paul's way of describing the likely outcome reveals his confidence in the power of prayer. He knew that specific prayers usually received definite answers; therefore, he encouraged persistent and particular prayer. His years of experience had convinced him of this reality, that prayer was essential in order for the kingdom to prosper.

A fourth quality that is obvious in this letter is Paul's *sacrificial leadership*. We can see this from his willingness to pay for any losses that Onesimus had caused Philemon (v. 18). Paul would not have had many resources; he does mention in Philippians the help that the church in Philippi had sent to him. Maybe he intended to use it to help Onesimus's case, or perhaps he had not yet received it from the Philippian church. The one thing he did know was that Onesimus, being a slave, had nothing and therefore no way of repaying any loss he had caused. But Paul was willing to pay it. In doing this he was like his Master, who had paid the higher debts of Paul and other believers. It is impossible to be a Christlike leader without this quality of sacrificial leadership. The sacrifice may be in terms of time, finance, or other aspects; there are many areas in which it can be displayed.

A fifth quality is Paul's *sensitive leadership*. Sensitivity can be both negative and positive. Negatively, it will include not saying something because our words may have hurtful consequences. Positively, it will include saying something because our words will bring encouragement. Paul engages in positive sensitivity when he describes other believers. In this letter he uses terms such as "brother," "fellow soldier," "fellow laborer," and "fellow prisoner." In doing so, he is an example of how to use words to bring encouragement to other believers, even though they did not have the same understanding of truth as he did or the wealth of experiences he had known.

A sixth quality is what we can call Paul's *shepherdlike leadership*. Recall the instructions that the risen Jesus gave to Peter at the Sea of Tiberius in John 21. The restored Peter was told to feed Christ's lambs and His sheep, with "lambs" referring to young or new Christians and "sheep" referring to older believers. In this letter we can see how Paul did both. He had given spiritual care to Onesimus, a new believer, and now he was giving spiritual counsel to Philemon, who was an established believer. And it is very striking how Paul deals with both types of believers with apparent ease.

A seventh quality is Paul's *selfless leadership*. We can see this feature in Paul's refusal to hold on to Onesimus and retain him to continue providing help during his imprisonment in Rome (v. 13). Clearly Paul thought highly of Onesimus and could have benefited from his presence. But as he looked at Onesimus and his changed life, the apostle saw that the former slave could provide great benefits for his master in Colosse. Therefore, Paul sent him away to Colosse. He was willing to give up what he could have kept; after all, he anticipated going to Colosse soon, and no one would have been surprised if he had suggested that Onesimus remain in Rome until the verdict connected to his future had been given. But for him to retain Onesimus would have been selfishness and not selflessness.

We can see from this letter that Paul did not have to be physically present to reveal his leadership qualities. And we see those qualities in all his letters. As far as his literary leadership role, it does not seem to matter if he was writing to a church or to an individual in an official or a private capacity; he was sensitive and strong, caring and challenging, encouraging and edifying in what he said.

Paul, as a leader in the church, knew the value of encouragement whether when received from others or when giving to others. In verse 21, he encourages Philemon by stating his confidence that Philemon would respond in a gracious manner to the demands expressed by Paul in his letter. And in verse 22, he encourages Philemon and the others in Colosse (the terms "your" and "you" in verse 22 are plural) to continue in prayer by reminding them that intercession for his deliverance would be effective because God answers prayer. A third aspect of encouragement is also seen in Paul's stated desire in verse 22 to have fellowship with Philemon at a future date when a visit to Colosse would be possible.

Pressing On

Often when we look at Paul, we feel overwhelmed by the strength of his resolve and the balance of his life. Yet Paul was also aware of his weaknesses, including, as far as his letter to Philemon was concerned, his old age (v. 9). That he mentioned his age indicates he was feeling the effects linked to it. Given the limited helps available at that time and the kind of stressful life he had lived, Paul must have had physical pain. He does mention that Luke is with him, whom he calls elsewhere "the beloved physician" (Col. 4:14), which suggests Paul's ongoing need of physical attention.

Yet Paul did not allow his advanced age and pain to inhibit his plans, and at the close of this letter, he mentions the possibility of traveling the many miles to Colosse from Rome should he be released. Whether he managed to get there is unknown, although he did travel widely between his two Roman imprisonments, as can be deduced from references in the Pastoral Epistles.

It is amazing to see the drive of this aged servant of Christ as he looks for further areas of service and usefulness. Perhaps it was feeling increasing physical limitations as well as the rapid passing of time that caused Paul to want to do more for his Master before the time came when he would not be able to do so. What is certain is that he was able to do what he did because God gave him strength

(Phil. 4:13). Paul as a leader was both diligent for God and dependent on God.

In his letters, Paul urges believers to follow his example as he followed the example of Jesus. His example of leadership has much to say to church leaders today as they aim to serve his Master in the roles that have been given to them for the benefit of the Christians and the churches that they have been called to serve.

19

What to Do with Onesimus?

PHILEMON 15–20

---

[15]For perhaps he departed for a while for this purpose, that you might receive him forever, [16]no longer as a slave but more than a slave—a beloved brother, especially to me but how much more to you, both in the flesh and in the Lord.

[17]If then you count me as a partner, receive him as you would me. [18]But if he has wronged you or owes anything, put that on my account. [19]I, Paul, am writing with my own hand. I will repay—not to mention to you that you owe me even your own self besides. [20]Yes, brother, let me have joy from you in the Lord; refresh my heart in the Lord.

In New Testament times, slavery was common throughout the Roman Empire and beyond, and that had been the case for centuries. It is estimated that half the population of the empire, about sixty million people, were slaves. People in what we today would regard as professional positions, such as doctors, lawyers, and managers, could be slaves. Many slaves were regarded as things by their owners. Changes were occurring slowly in the way that slaves could be treated, but everyday life had no concept of a world without slavery and would not for centuries to come. In many cases, the best that slaves could hope for was that they would be well cared for by their masters.

It was possible for a master to set slaves free, but unless those slaves had or attained resources of their own, life for them in such freedom would be very difficult. Slaves did run away from their masters, but there were severe penalties for this, including branding their forehead as fugitives and possible execution. Often, those who ran away became criminals since they had no other method of survival. Occasionally, there were large slave revolts, but they were crushed ruthlessly by the authorities.

Most free persons would have had slaves working in some way in their households. Slaves usually worked in the person's home, whether they served in the house or in fields or workshops connected to the house, and they would be regarded as members of the household, although at a lower level compared to the master's family.

The practice of slavery is relevant to this letter because Philemon owned at least one slave, Onesimus. Onesimus was not the only Christian slave in Colosse, nor was Philemon the only master with slaves, as we can see from Colossians 3:22–4:1:

> Bondservants, obey in all things your masters according to the flesh, not with eyeservice, as men-pleasers, but in sincerity of heart, fearing God. And whatever you do, do it heartily, as to the Lord and not to men, knowing that from the Lord you will receive the reward of the inheritance; for you serve the Lord Christ. But he who does wrong will be repaid for what he has done, and there is no partiality. Masters, give your bondservants what is just and fair, knowing that you also have a Master in heaven.

It is helpful to consider these words of Paul to the church in Colosse before thinking about the circumstances of Philemon and Onesimus.

What Paul Says to the Colossians

Basically, in the verses in Colossians, Paul tells both Christian slaves and Christian masters to realize at all times that they are serving the Lord. He has His eye on both of them all the time. Some Christian slaves would not have had Christian masters, and some Christian masters would not have had Christian slaves. (Onesimus had been a non-Christian slave in the household of Philemon, a Christian master.) Serving the Lord was a great privilege for both Christian slaves and Christian masters, with Paul mentioning that Christian slaves, who had nothing of their own in this world, would, if they served diligently, receive an eternal inheritance as their reward. Such service was also a great responsibility because both slaves and masters could fall short. Slaves could do so if they showed disrespect for their masters, and masters could do so if they behaved unjustly and unfairly toward their slaves.

What Paul is concerned with is inner transformation expressed in a world that could not imagine outer transformation of the practice of slavery. Society in the main could not conceive an external freedom from slavery that was beneficial, but Paul reminds his readers that hearts changed by the gospel show to society that a way of living exists that produces peace when everyone in a situation puts God first. His words are not intended to deal with finding ways of ending slavery as an external institution, whether by gradual design or by sudden change, but they are written to show how life can be God glorifying until the external circumstances are no longer the norm.

Centuries later, we live in a very different society, at least in theory. In most countries, slavery has been abolished, and we should be glad that is the case. Yet Paul's instructions that we should serve God wherever we are in society are still divine commands for Christians. And so also is his reminder that the location of true and total freedom is not in this world but in the eternal inheritance that can only be anticipated in the present and enjoyed in the future by responding now to the gospel offer of restoration to God's favor.

Onesimus

Onesimus had run away from his master Philemon. We are not told why he did so. Some speculate that he had gone to look for Paul in order for him to intervene in an issue concerning Philemon. That seems unlikely because Paul accepts that Onesimus previously had not been useful to Philemon (v. 11), and the basis of that opinion likely was connected to what Onesimus admitted after his conversion or to what Epaphras could have stated from previous contact with Onesimus in Colosse.

Rather, Onesimus was a runaway slave hoping to hide among the population in Rome. He came into contact with Paul by unknown means and through that contact was converted. Paul may not have been in a literal prison but perhaps was a prisoner under guard in his own accommodation (Acts 28:16, 30–31). Clearly, Onesimus had talents and was able to help Paul quickly to such an extent that the apostle wanted his service to continue. Yet that could not happen without Philemon's permission.

Paul does not seem to have reported Onesimus to the authorities, which reveals his sympathy for slaves in their plight and also a determination to avoid the fierce punishment that could have been given to Onesimus. Instead, he encouraged Onesimus to return to Philemon and sent an accompanying letter with appropriate advice for dealing with the situation, including a description of the "new" Onesimus for Philemon to ponder. The willingness of Onesimus to go reveals the profound way in which his outlook had been changed by God's grace. He was willing to let his future be decided by Philemon, the master who had been wronged.

Philemon

How was Philemon to deal with the situation? Paul's advice is connected to the doctrine of adoption, which he applies in various ways in verses 15–20. First, Philemon and Onesimus now have a permanent relationship, not merely the temporary one of bondservant and master. Because Onesimus has become a Christian, he and Philemon are now brothers in the family of God. Paul observes that he is also a beloved brother of Onesimus, but the conversion of Onesimus should mean even more to Philemon because of the human contact they had previously when they lived in the same household.

Second, Paul informs Philemon that since Onesimus is his brother, he should give him his freedom (v. 16). While Paul does not spell out what Onesimus would do when freed, the implication, based on Paul's estimation of Onesimus, is that he would help Paul in some way in his ministry labors. It would be easier for Onesimus to do so if he had such freedom to travel as a free person. Paul could be stressing that Onesimus should no longer be Philemon's slave at the human level.

Third, Paul urges Philemon, as his partner in ministry, to recognize that Onesimus is now also such a partner (v. 17). While there would be more to such a recognition than showing hospitality, we can see from later in the letter that Paul expected his partner Philemon to provide for his needs when he would come to Colosse (v. 21). Onesimus would also have needs, and he should be given a brother's welcome when he reached Colosse.

Fourth, as a brother, Paul offers to make amends to brother Philemon for any losses he experienced when his new brother Onesimus ran away (vv. 17–18). The apostle was aware that Philemon owed much to him because it was probably through him that Philemon had become a Christian (v. 19). It would be difficult for Philemon to insist on reparation from Onesimus in the light of Paul's reasoning about recognizing one's personal indebtedness to divine grace.

Fifth, Paul desired Philemon to provide spiritual refreshment by exhibiting brotherly love for Onesimus. This is a legitimate benefit to expect because all believers, especially those serving Jesus in difficult circumstances, long for encouragement in their ministry. Paul had expectations for Onesimus, but they would only be realized if Philemon met Paul's expectations for him. We might think that Paul was asking something hard, but should it have been difficult for Philemon, a pardoned sinner, to forgive his former slave, who was now his brother and recognized by Paul as suitable for Christian service?

20

Learning from Paul's Contacts

PHILEMON 23–24

---

[23]*Epaphras, my fellow prisoner in Christ Jesus, greets you,* [24]*as do Mark, Aristarchus, Demas, Luke, my fellow laborers.*

When we are away from home and write to say how things are, we will sometimes mention who is with us, whether it is work colleagues or other friends and contacts. At the very least, their presence will let those at home know that we are not alone. Paul chooses to let Philemon know that five people are with him. We may wonder why those names are mentioned in God's Word, and one answer is that they show us who we can imitate and who we should not imitate. We can look at the details given about these men and see what we can learn from them about serving Jesus.

Epaphras

The first person Paul mentions is Epaphras, who is mentioned only in the book of Colossians and in the letter to Philemon. He was from Colosse, and he had been the person who had taken the gospel there (Col. 1:7). So he would have known Philemon well, especially since some, if not all, of the Christians in Colosse met in his home for worship services. At the time of the writing of Philemon, Epaphras was a prisoner alongside Paul. We are not told how he became a prisoner.

In Colossians 1:7, Epaphras is called a *faithful* minister on behalf of the Colossians. This has two possible meanings: first, he was faithful in the sense that he had conveyed the truth (this could be Paul's endorsement of Epaphras's teaching), or, second, it could mean that he was faithful in the sense that he had carried out a task on behalf of the church (perhaps the Colossians were wondering why Epaphras was taking so long to return).

Why did Epaphras serve in this way? Paul gives the answer when he calls him a "fellow servant" (literally, a "fellow slave") of Jesus Christ (Col. 1:7; see also 4:12). Epaphras recognized that he was owned by Jesus. This is a reminder that Jesus has purchased us for Himself, and we show that we recognize this reality by doing everything He tells us to do. As far as Epaphras was concerned, every aspect of his personality was devoted to Jesus, his Master.

Epaphras also showed fidelity toward others. He was loyal to Christ, to Paul, and to the Colossians. Paul had entrusted Epaphras with taking the gospel to Colosse, and he had not betrayed that confidence. Furthermore, he was steadfast concerning the good things that were going on in the Colossian congregation; he told Paul about their "love in the Spirit" (Col. 1:8). Epaphras delighted to tell others about the Colossians' growth in grace.

Paul also says that Epaphras was working hard for those in Colosse, Hierapolis, and Laodicea, locations near to each other, by praying zealously for them (Col. 4:12–13). His prayer involved toil and persistence; indeed, Paul says that Epaphras labored fervently in prayer. There is an allusion to wrestling in that description. With whom was Epaphras wrestling? He was struggling with God even as Jacob had done at Peniel. Yet there is one difference at least. Jacob wrestled with God for a night; Epaphras was wrestling all the time.

In what ways did Epaphras wrestle in prayer? I have just mentioned one aspect—his constancy in praying. Persistence in anything requires great energy. Another detail is the coverage of his praying: he embraced people in three cities. He struggled on behalf of those he knew. In this regard, Epaphras is a challenge to us in our prayer lives.

Mark

The other four people Paul mentions are described as his fellow workers. Mark, also called John, was a relation of Barnabas, a man with whom Paul had once worked very closely. Sadly, disagreement over Mark was the reason why Barnabas and Paul had ceased working together. During Paul's first missionary journey, Barnabas and Paul had taken Mark as a helper, but he gave up before the journey was completed and returned home to Jerusalem (Acts 13:13).

Later, when Paul planned to revisit the churches founded on that journey, Barnabas wanted to take Mark with them. Paul refused because of the way Mark had behaved previously (Acts 15:36-41). Clearly, Paul had not seen any change in Mark that would allow him to participate in the next missionary journey. This refusal brought about an estrangement between Paul and Barnabas. Barnabas went to Cyprus with Mark, whereas Paul took Silas with him on his second missionary journey.

At some point Mark rejoined Paul. We don't know when, but obviously he was with Paul during his imprisonment. Paul later also wanted Mark to join him in his future and final imprisonment: "Get Mark and bring him with you, for he is useful to me for ministry" (2 Tim. 4:11). Mark had failed initially, but Paul now regarded him as useful.

Mark is an example of someone who failed but was later recognized for his worth. Paul even mentions the possibility that Mark would pass through Colosse at some stage (Col. 4:10). And we know that he did not serve just the first-century church. He also served the church of the future when he wrote his gospel. Even that detail points to the grace of God when He gave Mark this privilege and guided him as he wrote it. Mark is a challenge to us as to how we deal with our failures and accept the Lord's restoring discipline.

Aristarchus

If he is the same person who is mentioned in Acts 19:29; 20:4; and 27:2, Aristarchus was from Macedonia. He was one of the men who accompanied Paul to Jerusalem when he delivered the great collection that he had gathered to help the church there. This trip would have its dangers because of people trying to rob them of the collection, although God prevented that from happening. But Aristarchus was willing to go. Paul was arrested in Jerusalem, and that began the process by which he reached Rome as a prisoner. Aristarchus accompanied him on that journey.

In Colossians 4:10, Aristarchus is described as Paul's fellow prisoner, whereas Epaphras is mentioned as a bondservant of Christ, perhaps indicating he was not a prisoner at that time (Col. 4:12). In the letter to Philemon, Epaphras is described as a prisoner, and Aristarchus is not. The suggestion has been made that they took turns, as it were, to volunteer to be with Paul the prisoner, an option that was available to friends of prisoners. If that is the case, then we can see that Aristarchus was willing to share Paul's suffering in a very practical way.

We do not know what else Aristarchus did as a fellow worker of Paul in the service of the Master. But we can see from those two details that he challenges us about how we ought to alleviate need. He was willing to travel a long distance to help the needy church in Jerusalem, and he was willing to sit with Paul in his imprisonment and help him.

Demas

Demas is the sad example in this list. Like the others, he is mentioned in the letter to the Colossians and in the letter to Philemon as being with Paul and sending greetings to the recipients. Clearly, he was interested in the things of the kingdom at that time, even though Paul was imprisoned. Yet the other reference to him, which occurs a few years later during Paul's second Roman imprisonment, tells a very different story because Paul says in 2 Timothy 4:10 that "Demas has forsaken me, having loved this present world, and has departed for Thessalonica."

Demas challenges us regarding the possibility that we may lose our zeal and abandon our commitment to the Savior's kingdom. One difference between the two imprisonments was that Paul expected to be released from the first (Phil. 1:19–26) and was condemned to die in the second (2 Tim. 4:6). Perhaps Demas could not cope with the possibility of martyrdom and put living in this world before serving Jesus. And is that not a real challenge in today's world?

Luke

Of the five people mentioned in the list, Luke is the only one whose employment is known; he was a physician. He also wrote two books of the New Testament—his gospel and the book of Acts. Luke first appears in the book of Acts when Paul leaves Troas to go to Macedonia.[1] Later on, he was with Paul when he took the collection that he had gathered to Jerusalem and then remained with him for the prolonged period of his trials after his arrest. Maybe that was when Luke gathered the information about Jesus included in his gospel. Then he went with Paul to Rome for his first imprisonment. He was also with Paul during his second imprisonment; indeed, he was the only one who was with him (2 Tim. 4:11).

In what ways does Luke challenge us? Perhaps he used his medical skills to help Paul in his physical troubles. What is clear about Luke is his faithfulness and his reliability. He was firm in his devotion.

Application to Us

Obviously, those men were with Paul through divine providence. But then so are the friends and companions we have. It is good to choose as friends those who will help us in our walk with God. No doubt, those men encouraged one another in service for Christ. Yet it was sad that one of them gave up his faith a few years later when the going became really tough. This was a great disappointment, no

1. In Acts 16:10–11, Luke uses the first-person plural to describe those making the journey, indicating that he was one of the travelers. When Paul and his companions move on from Philippi, Luke uses the third-person plural (Acts 16:40), indicating that he does not go with them. A few years later, Paul returns to Philippi, and when he leaves, Luke goes with him (Acts 20:5–6) and remains with him in his subsequent travels until he reaches Rome for his trial.

doubt, to Paul. Our resolve, through God's grace, must be to pray like Epaphras, repent like Mark, be helpful to the needy like Aristarchus, and be faithful like Luke. And we must pray and watch that we do not imitate Demas.

21

The Grace of Our Lord Jesus Christ Be with Your Spirit

PHILEMON 25

---

[25] *The grace of our Lord Jesus Christ be with your spirit. Amen.*

We are accustomed to benedictions that refer to the three persons of the Trinity and may be surprised to discover that there is not a biblical requirement that the three persons should always be mentioned. In Romans 15:13, Paul gives a benediction in which the Father and the Holy Spirit are mentioned, and in Romans 15:33 he gives another in which only the Father is mentioned. Usually, his letters open with a benediction that mentions the Father and the Son.

This is not the only occasion in which the second person of the Trinity is the divine person who is mentioned. Paul uses similar benedictions in Romans 16:20; Galatians 6:18; Philippians 4:23; and 1 Thessalonians 5:28. So we can deduce that Paul used this benediction frequently throughout his ministry.

Before we look into the meaning of this benediction, we will observe three obvious points. One is that Paul thought that Philemon needed this spiritual experience in order to face what was coming his way. The second is that Paul knew this grace was available for Philemon. The third is that Paul knew this grace was suitable for Philemon, whatever he was going through.

The Dignity of Jesus

There is another question we might ask: Why does Paul not say, "The grace of God the Son be with you"? He may not have had a special reason for not doing so. Nevertheless, we may ask why he uses this description of Jesus. I suggest that Paul's reason is connected to how we think about the second person of the Trinity. In giving this name to Him, Paul is urging us to remember that Jesus is the Mediator between God and man and that He became a man in order to provide us with the blessings and benefits of salvation God planned to give to us.

In order to be the Mediator, Jesus has to be able to represent the two parties involved—God and man. As the Son of God, a divine person possessing all the attributes of God and always fully cognizant of the plans of God, He can represent God perfectly. Moreover, He is a real man, fully able to represent His people at the same time as He represents God and to do so perfectly. While He had never lived in Colosse, He knew what it was like to live in Colosse and what degree of divine grace Philemon needed.

There is a wonderful picture of Jesus as our representative in the way that the high priest of Israel carried the names of the twelve tribes into the presence of God. The names were on his shoulders, which is the place of strength, and on his breastplate, which is the place of affections. We should remind ourselves frequently of this great reality that we have such a Mediator.

We can say more about Jesus as Mediator through this statement because it includes the title "Lord," which is a reminder to us of the position He now enjoys in heaven. Forty days after His resurrection, He ascended to heaven and took His place at the right hand of God and was given the title "Lord." In His person as the Son of God, He was always Lord. Yet when He became man, His lordship was hidden from people's eyes, and most who saw Him had no idea who He was. But the great day of His coronation came at His ascension when public acknowledgment was made in the highest location that the one who had suffered on the cross for sinners has been highly exalted and given the name "Lord."

This means that whenever we repeat this benediction, we are making a great confession. We affirm with great joy that He is the appointed King of the universe, the one who has all power in heaven and on earth. And not only are we affirming His status, but we are also affirming His competence to fulfill the spiritual needs of His people wherever they are.

The Determination of Jesus

It may help us understand this benediction better if we think briefly about another verse that describes the grace of Jesus. Paul writes in 2 Corinthians 8:9: "For you know the grace of our Lord Jesus Christ, that though He was rich, yet for your sakes He became poor, that you through His poverty might become rich." This verse indicates that the purpose of His death was so we could share His riches.

While many details can be deduced from this verse, two are of relevance for us as we consider Paul's benediction about the grace of the Lord Jesus Christ. The first is the intensity of His desire that we become rich. We can measure a person's intensity for something by the lengths to which he or she will go to attain it. A person who wants to win an Olympic medal will focus his attention on being ready for the attempt. The heart of Jesus was focused on liberating His people from sin and its consequences, which He did by suffering on the cross as their substitute when He bore the wrath of God against their sins. We should always admire the intensity of Jesus as He went to the cross.

The second detail to observe in this verse is the generosity of Jesus. We can estimate whether or not people are generous by comparing their giving to their resources. A multimillionaire who gives ten pounds to a beggar is not being generous. Generous people do not give out of their resources but *according to* their resources. Jesus does not merely give out of His resources, but He makes His people rich according to His estimation. The obvious deduction we can make is that grace will be given in abundance.

There is another detail that we must remember as we think about this connection to the grace of Jesus, and Peter mentions it in 2 Peter 3:18: "But grow in the grace and knowledge of our Lord and Savior Jesus Christ." Peter indicates the exclusiveness of the grace of Jesus as the location of Christian progress—we cannot develop in a spiritual way anywhere else. And Peter also highlights the similarity between growing in grace and growing in knowledge of Jesus. His words tell us that experiencing the grace of Jesus will involve getting to know Jesus better, and we will think about some of those ways now.

The Delight of Jesus

Jesus wants each of His people to know Him intimately, and the only way that they can know Him is through His grace. We know that the subject of His grace is vast, and we need to break it down into different areas. Yet as we break it down, we must remind ourselves that doing so enables us to know Jesus more deeply than previously.

One way to look at His grace is to remind ourselves that it is *purchased grace*. We have already thought about this aspect when reflecting on Paul's words in 2 Corinthians 8:9. Yet it is important for us to realize and to remind ourselves that the giving of grace is certain. I may know a person who can help me, but that is different from knowing that he or she will help me. How do I know that Jesus will give grace to each of His people? Because He purchased it for them. We know that He commenced showing grace to them before they thought of asking Him about it when He started the process of bringing them to Himself through the gospel.

Another way to look at the grace of Jesus is to remind ourselves that it is *plentiful grace*. It is plentiful in degree as well as in extent. Without looking at particular aspects, we can see that His grace covers all the areas of spiritual needs of every believer and lasts throughout that person's life on earth. How many are experiencing His grace at the moment throughout the world? Millions and millions. I suppose each of us could easily create a list of ways in which the grace of Jesus has been given to us. Because it is plentiful, it means that we do not have to worry that somehow it will run out. Jesus is always full of grace.

At the same time, we have to remember that it is *personal grace* in the sense that Jesus ensures that each of His people receives the particular grace they need at any given time. This is a reminder of

His awareness of and interest in His people. They probably pray for grace often and may have a particular kind in mind. Yet the Savior knows exactly the kind of grace they will require, and He provides it for each of them in their own personal way.

Those three aspects of grace—purchased, plentiful, and personal—describe it in general. While it is good to look at grace from a general perspective, it is also beneficial for us to look at it in special ways. One special way is to consider *pardoning grace*, which is one that each of God's people need on innumerable occasions. How often we need this purchased, plentiful, and personal grace! The fact that it is purchased means that it will be given, the fact that it is plentiful means that it will be given always, and the fact that it is personal means that it will be given accurately and meaningfully for each of His people.

A second form of particular grace is what we can call *provided grace*, in the sense of His people receiving from Jesus His choice of spiritual food for their souls. The reality is that only heavenly food will satisfy the new creature. Even things that are not necessarily sinful will not fully satisfy our regenerated souls. The only spiritual food that will satisfy our hearts is Jesus Himself, and this may be why Peter told us to grow in grace and in the knowledge of Jesus. Unlike the best of earthly food, Jesus does not become uninteresting if we have such a diet every day. And speaking of diets, we don't need to worry about any bad growth appearing as a consequence of feeding on Christ. There is enough in the person and work of Jesus to satisfy the largest of minds, the strongest of emotions, and the most determined of searchers.

Then a third form of particular grace is *peculiar grace*, by which I mean experiencing grace in unusual ways. One common example is the way that believers in trouble can enjoy the peace of God, sometimes in very difficult or dangerous situations. They may be facing trials that look severe, but during them they can have an amazing sense of the Lord's presence. This experience is beyond human explanation, but it is a common way by which believers come to know Jesus in a deeper way. As Samuel Rutherford said in one of his letters, "O, what I owe to the file, to the hammer, to the furnace of my Lord Jesus!"

A fourth way in which Jesus comes in grace to His people is by what we can call *prospective grace*, by which I mean that He gives to them foretastes of and assurance about the heavenly homeland. Such grace is given through descriptions of heaven in the Bible, but they become so precious through the hidden working of the Spirit as He seems to whisper in our souls, "This is where you are heading." I see no reason why we should not read a verse or a chapter about heaven every day. As has often been suggested, an heir to an inheritance will often think about the day it will be his and the benefits it will bring to him.

I mention a fifth kind of grace from Jesus that I call *preventing grace*. This is given to stop us succumbing to Satan's temptations or to our own sinful tendencies. Are you ever surprised that you did not lose your temper in a difficult situation? The achievement was not arrived at through your abilities but through the grace of Jesus preventing you from sinning. There are many examples that could be given of this wonderful aspect of grace.

So we can say that Paul has a great deal in mind when he refers to the grace of the Lord Jesus Christ. Philip Henry preached a sermon on this text a year before he died, and his son Matthew commented on it:

> Now the choicest gift we can ask of God for our friends is, that this *grace of our Lord Jesus Christ* may *be with their spirit*. This is "the one thing needful, the better part, the root of the matter, the whole man, the principle thing, the more excellent way, a blessing indeed, and the thing that accompanies salvation." The grace of Christ in the spirit enlightens and enlivens the spirit, softens and subdues the spirit, purifies and preserves the spirit, greatens and guides the spirit, sweetens and strengthens the spirit; and therefore, what can be more desirable?[1]

1. *The Miscellaneous Works of the Rev. Matthew Henry* (London: Joseph Ogle Robinson, 1833), 1:118–19.